Mary Berwick,
A colleague in the service of
peace and justice
George Ricker

What You Don't Have to Believe to Be a Christian

D0880262

George M. Ricker

SUNBELT EAKIN · Austin, Texas

To
Frances
Cherished companion and confidante
without whose persistence
this book would never
have been
written.

Love, if you knew the light
That your soul casts in my sight,
How I look to you
For the pure and the true
And the beauteous and the right . . .
—Robert Browning

Contents

Foreword

You might expect a book called *What You Don't Have to Believe to Be a Christian* to belong to that old American genre of "debunking"—to take the nonsense out of something. But George Ricker escapes that category by walking the most delicate of lines between loving respect for every article of literal belief a dutiful Christian might be lugging on the long journey home and unwavering commitment to telling the truth as he has experienced it. Not once do you feel that triumphant note of the intellectual facing the mysteries of faith and going with hoe and spade to chop and dig the nonsense out of it.

And yet this book is deeply intellectual, scorning neither faith nor the mind that questions faith. The style is clear, straightforward, and true in the sense that measuring devices are "true." We trust this person talking, who is simply talking, earnestly, but not selling anything or defensively upholding a beleaguered tradition. Those who enter the book with beliefs in the virgin birth, the miracles, the literal resurrection of the body, and other religious treasures will not be lectured to set them down and travel more lightly.

Believers will leave the book feeling lucky to have their beliefs. And for the one or two beliefs that they may have struggled to maintain, Ricker offers assurance that perhaps they don't have to struggle quite so hard to hold on—it's not all-or-nothing when it comes to believing.

But the true value of the book is for outsiders to Christianity: for those who can look at believers with incredulity that any thinking person in the twenty-first century can believe what Christians are said to believe; or for those who left the church as they dropped one belief after another, until they felt they were no longer welcome there—and might no longer be Christians. For outsiders, Ricker does not offer the easy comfort of a shared intellectual superiority—he does not pander to doubt. He simply clears the field of all the clutter of distracting literalisms until what is left shines out so clearly that faith seems more obviously true than doubt.

Faith, Ricker points out, is not the same as belief. Many of the hard-to-believe stories Christians tell operate at a level of truth that is deeper than fact. Faith is not the product of reason, but it's not irrational. This point is made in as many different ways as there are chapters in the book. If absolute, literal beliefs form an intellectual barrier against the expanded life Christianity offers, the journey through Ricker's book allows us to drop these beliefs, one by one. With the road cleared of intellectual stumbling blocks, what is left, in the end, is a clear path toward the "one thing needful" on the journey—the *experience* of the *presence* of God.

—Betty Sue Flowers, Ph.D.

Preface

What You Don't Have to Believe to Be a Christian

Is this a presumptuous statement? No. I am a Christian, and the chapters contain what I do not believe. Other Christians may believe some, much, or all of the statements that begin the chapters. I simply make the claim that a Christian does not have to; for, in spite of all my disbeliefs, I am a committed Christian.

How, then, do I define the word *Christian*? A Christian is one for whom Jesus Christ plays the definitive role in life. In one way or another the man of Nazareth determines one's identity, helps to define what it means to be human, and offers the assurance of a source of eternal love available to each human being.

However, many Christians live with doubts about much that they have heard about Christianity, and they feel guilty. Some may go so far as to think that whatever is believed by many Christians should be believed by all. Not so! Bishop J. A. T. Robinson has put it well: "[A]s one goes on, it is the things one doesn't believe and finds one doesn't have to believe which are as liberating as the things one does."[1] I am convinced that he is right.

Others have been turned off by Christianity and the Church by beliefs that seem to be absurd and anti-intellectual. They become part of some so-called "free-thinking" movement that, while encouraging the use of the mind, misses the profundity of the symbolic and mythological dimensions of the Christian faith. They do not realize that much that falls under the rubric of beliefs is not taken as literal or historical truth by all Christians.

What follows flows out of my years as a pastor and teacher. I have observed the exhilaration of individuals who have discovered that it is all right to think, to question, and even to doubt much that has been believed. Such doubting and questioning may not be acceptable to some Christians who insist on doctrinal conformity, but that is their problem and not mine. Doctrinal rigidity is holding fast to what has been believed by many Christians in times past but which is now questioned because of changes in cosmology and anthropology as well as linguistic, philosophical, and historical studies.

The disbeliefs that head each chapter are followed by personal and existential meanings that go beyond literalism. Not believing does not necessarily mean not affirming. How hard it is for some to see that not believing the literal and historical accuracy of some statement is not denying a deeper dimension of truth behind the affirmation. Furthermore, each affirmation is subject to exploration in order to mine significant insights into the faith once given to the saints. I am simply stating that believing in everything as literal or historical truth is not only not necessary but may hide the deeper truths behind the traditional language. If your mind does not so function, then you are, of course, free to continue to accept as historical what others cannot.

This book is designed to open the dialogue on issues about which many Christian have doubts. Some will accuse me of hurting the "babes in Christ." I cannot guarantee that no one will be disturbed by the contents of this book. I can assert that many "babes in Christ" remain babes because the Church and its clergy have been silent on many of these issues. If babes are to grow up and be nurtured by solid food, then they must put aside the pabulum and chew some meat. Many have left the Church because they were not receiving the substance of the gospel. The raising of questions and doubting of long-held beliefs are preludes to a more mature faith. Such a faith is not based on unnatural and miraculous happenings. This faith relies on the life of one who disturbed the traditional beliefs of his time in order to present a more creative, unifying, compassionate, and inclusive faith for those who would follow him. I claim to be one of those, irrespective of questioning many traditional beliefs. I remain excited by being in a community of learning and growing that prepares the way for that realm of God proclaimed by Jesus.

For those with never a doubt, these chapters may produce some disturbance at the least, or outright anger. I respectfully request that you consider seriously the reason for your response and ask yourself what benefit ensues from believing what the mind tells you is unbelievable. To those who find what I have to say to be provocative and freeing, no further word is necessary.

Gratitude is due to many groups and individuals with whom I have shared the ideas presented here. Groups include the Crusaders, Upper Room, and Jack Hughes Sunday school classes at First United Methodist Church in San Marcos, Texas; the Downtowners, Oasis, New Visions, Faith Builders, and Becomers classes at First United Methodist Church in Austin; the Couples Plus, Odyssey, Renaissance, Questors, and New Wesley classes at University United Methodist Church in Austin; the Discovery Class at First United Methodist Church in Georgetown, Texas; two four-week classes at Wednesday Community Nights at University

United Methodist; a five-week class at Wednesday Night Live at First United Methodist in Georgetown; a class of ninety at Encuentro (a Southwest Texas Conference education program) in San Antonio; and a four-week series at Tuesday Night Live at St. John's United Methodist Church in Austin; two sessions for the Forum Class at St. David's Episcopal Church in Austin; and three sessions for the Men's Breakfast at Good Shepherd Episcopal Church in Austin. In addition I have taught much of this material in a continuing-education program at the University of Texas (SAGE—Seminars for Adult Growth and Enrichment)—two six-week sessions meeting once a week. At all of these, the laypeople and a few clergy were engaged and enthusiastically responsive and, by their questioning, helped me to clarify much of this material. In addition, Bill Fuller at the Campus Christian Community in San Marcos gave valuable assistance by placing my chalkboard charts on the computer. Also, I am grateful to Julian Martin and Charles Moore who read the manuscript and offered many helpful suggestions. Last but foremost, I am grateful to my wife, Frances, for her counsel, honest feed-back, and dogged insistence that I finish this project.

—George M. Ricker

Introduction

The chapters that follow contain much about which Christians disagree. In order to understand what a Christian does not have to believe, this introduction is crucial. I urge you, therefore, to give these pages careful attention.

What do Christians believe? Many things! And sometimes our beliefs are hard to talk about. Beliefs can get very personal, so that we are reluctant to express ourselves. We are aware of the old adage to the effect that if we want to live in harmony, we should avoid two subjects: politics and religion. This reluctance to express one's beliefs is illustrated in the story of George Whitefield, one of the early preachers in the Wesleyan revivals in England and Scotland, who confronted a Scotsman:

"What do you believe?" Whitefield questioned.

"What my church believes," was the response.

"What does your church believe?" Whitefield persisted.

"What I believe," asserted the Scotsman.

"What do you both believe?" he questioned in exasperation.

"The same thing," retorted the Scotsman.

Here at the beginning we need to differentiate between belief and faith. A belief is that to which we give intellectual assent. A belief may or may not have any bearing upon our actions. About 90 percent of the people in our country believe in the existence of God, according to the polls, but we cannot assert that the belief affects the way of life of that 90 percent. We can stand by the deep end of a swimming pool and assert, "I believe I can swim," but such belief is not swimming. Faith is what we trust in, what we rely upon, what we are committed to, and what we are willing to base our lives upon. Belief is inactive and changes to faith when we are willing to jump in the water and trust that by going through the proper motions the water will support us. In like fashion, belief in God becomes faith when we are willing to base our lives on the presence of unbounded love and trust that in whatever happens, in the words of the psalmist, we are being held by God's right hand. (Ps. 73:21)

What Christians Believe about Jesus

What do Christians believe about Jesus? Again, many things. If we ask the question "Who was (is) Jesus?" we get the traditional response: "He is the Son of God." Beware of such traditional answers. A second question needs to be asked: "What does that mean?" To that query we find myriad answers. But first, where did the term *Son of God* originate? From the Jewish Scriptures! The Davidic kings were called sons of God. In 2 Samuel 7:12–15, Solomon is called God's son. In Psalm 2:7, a coronation hymn, the decree of the Lord is "You are my son, today I have begotten you." Such is the Davidic king. In this context, the centurion at the cross said, "Truly this man was a Son of God." (Mark 15:39 NEB)

Other testimonies to the divinity of Jesus are given in the Gospels. In Mark, at Jesus' baptism, the words come, "You are my beloved Son; with you I am well pleased."

(Mark 1:11) In Matthew and Luke we find the stories of the virgin birth complete with angels, star, shepherds, and wise men. Paul, in Romans, asserts that Jesus is Son of God by his resurrection from the dead (Romans 1:4). And in both John 1 and Philippians 2:5–11, Jesus is referred to as the pre-existent Son.

What do these various testimonies mean? What happened to lead the writers of the Christian Scriptures to make such assertions? How did dogma develop? Experience precedes dogma. Something happens, and then people talk about it. What happened to people in their relationship with Jesus and in their memory of him? People were changed, reconciled, given hope, empowered, and energized. How could they understand this? Their experience told them that this was of God, from God; and they had to give testimony to that experience using the language and thought forms of their time. "Son of God" was the title they chose to confer on Jesus. They felt that the term was appropriate, and I do, too; but the reality behind the term is shrouded in mystery.

Metaphors for What Jesus Does for Us

If we were to ask the further question "What does Jesus do for us?" we would get another traditional answer: "He saves us." Again, the second question needs to be asked: "What does that mean?" The cross is the primary symbol of the atonement theories in the Christian faith. What the cross means cannot be expressed in such a way that every Christian is satisfied. From the early Christians until now, explanations have varied tremendously. The Christian Scriptures have at least six salvation (atonement) metaphors. Note the diagram on page 4 with each metaphor pointing to one meaning found in the crucifixion.

The language of sacrifice comes, of course, from the Hebrew sacrificial system. A lamb was slain and its blood

Salvation (Atonement) Metaphors

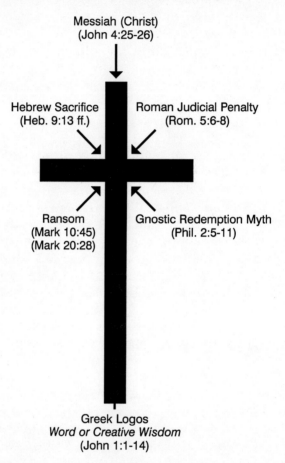

Messiah (Christ)
(John 4:25-26)

Hebrew Sacrifice
(Heb. 9:13 ff.)

Roman Judicial Penalty
(Rom. 5:6-8)

Ransom
(Mark 10:45)
(Mark 20:28)

Gnostic Redemption Myth
(Phil. 2:5-11)

Greek Logos
Word or Creative Wisdom
(John 1:1-14)

Notes:

1) All are metaphors. Each is saying: "It is as though ..."
2) Each is borrowed language from the culture of that day.
3) None of these is absolute. Each one is a pointer emerging out of the experience of new life.

sprinkled on the people. Blood was and is a symbol of life.The slain animal's blood united them in one life as the People of God. We do not live with such a symbol today, and many question whether this language is helpful in pointing us to what Jesus does for us. The statement in 1 Peter 1:2 that we are "to be sprinkled with his blood" is a metaphor of another day and hardly one we have to use.

The first Christians proclaimed that Jesus was the Messiah and called him the Christ, the Greek translation of the Hebrew word for Messiah. Jesus was uncomfortable with this designation, which is obvious from a study of the Gospels. His preferred self-designation was the term "Son of Man," which may have meant simply a human being or representative man, or could be related to the heavenly being in the non-canonical book Enoch. In any case, Jesus may have resisted the term "Messiah" because of its political orientation. The expected Jewish Messiah, the anointed Davidic king, was to be a political and military figure who would bring back the nation of Israel to its time of prominence under David. Jesus rejected this concept of a Messiah and seemed to identify more with the suffering servant of Isaiah 53. Except for those who are expecting Jesus to return as a military ruler, most Christians have accepted the term "Christ" as the reconciling activity of God represented in Jesus and focused in self-sacrificial and suffering love. The Messiah, or Christ, is a metaphorical term for the one hoped for, who would bring new life to the People of God. Jesus was called the Christ because he put an end to the Messiah quest. In Jesus, fullness or life, wholeness of life, has come among us, and in his coming he empowers us to live in like fashion.

The early church also used judicial language in asserting that Jesus paid the penalty for our sins. What this says to us is that some early Christians experienced being set free from the judgment of not being right (unrighteous). They were acutely aware of the Roman judicial system of justice and chose to put their experience in judicial terms. Before the judgment seat of God, they were in the wrong; but Jesus, who was free from guilt, paid the penalty with his life. What a powerful metaphor! But when pressed, questions arise. What are we guilty of, and is it sufficient for the death penalty? Is God the stern and righteous judge who demands the penalty of death? Jesus does not present God in such a fashion in the Gospels. And what is the rationale for one man paying the penalty for all of humanity? Yes, I have heard some of the answers to all these questions, but, frankly, they are not satisfying to me.

At the same time, this judicial metaphor has had a powerful influence on the Christian community. Grady Hardin, who pastored a church in Houston and later became a professor of worship at Perkins School of Theology, told me some years ago of his sermon entitled "Christian Gunsmoke." In short, the sermon focused on a man who murdered and robbed another. He was caught, tried, and sentenced to be hanged by the neck until he was dead. On the morning of the hanging, the murderer was taken to "hanging tree" and placed on a horse. The noose was placed around his neck. Just as they were about to strike the horse, Matt Dillon rode to the criminal's side, took off the noose, placed it on his own neck, struck the horse, and was hanged. He took the penalty upon himself; he became a substitute. The criminal was set free to live a different life. He had been died for. Sound bizarre? The tale is, in modern dress, the judicial theory or metaphor of the atonement. Does this really explain what Jesus did for us? Or is this one among many attempts of the early Christians to communicate their experience in the language of their day?

Still another metaphor is common language among Christians. Jesus was a divine being who lived in another realm of existence and came to earth to do for us what we could not do for ourselves. This is characteristic imagery from the gnostics, a philosophical sect identified by Church fathers as purveyors of Greek wisdom. Other authorities have referred to gnosticism as pre-Christian oriental mysticism. The gnostics had a plan of salvation involving both a cosmic and a historical drama. In the gnostic redemption myth, a heaven-sent redeemer comes to enact in his own life the cycle of suffering, dying, and rising again. Paul, as noted in Philippians 2:5–11, was trained in Greek ways of thinking and found this imagery helpful in presenting the Christian story. He used borrowed language to testify to what Jesus had accomplished in his suffering, death, and resurrection. Again we are looking at the use of thought forms from the world of that day to express what had been experienced. Jesus was from God, suffered and died for us, and in the resurrection event offers us a new life. Is this an absolute, the only way to express the experience of salvation? Not so. This is one of a number of ways of communicating the good news and is more or less helpful depending on one's own experience and mental processes.

Yet another metaphor is related to the last one and comes also from Greek philosophy. Jesus is the Logos of God enfleshed. The Greek word *logos* is used in the Gospel of John and is translated by the term *Word. Logos* in Greek philosophy is the divine wisdom which brought the world into being and is still involved in the world's becoming. Heraclitus used the term *logos* to describe ultimate reality. *Wisdom* in the Hebrew Scriptures is a synonym for God. John's Gospel couples Greek philosophy with the wisdom tradition of the Hebrew Scriptures to give a different testimony to what was experienced in the life and death of Jesus. In Jesus was the incarnation or enfleshment of the divine wisdom that created the world. This creative wisdom of God was God in action in the life, death, and resurrection of Jesus to bring light into a dark world. Again, we find borrowed language, this time from Greek philosophy, to proclaim an experienced reality.

One other metaphor remains with which all Christians

are familiar. Jesus paid the ransom for our sin. It is as though we have been kidnapped by Satan (more about Satan in a later chapter) and are being held for ransom. And what is the ransom? The life of God's Son. We have been set free from our captivity by God's free gift of God's Son. Again, a powerful symbol used both in Mark 10:25 and Matthew 20:28, but a metaphor. Is this to be taken literally? Did Satan kidnap humanity? Is Jesus' life literally a ransom paid, or is this some early Christians' borrowing of the language of their day to testify to their experience of new life and freedom?

Consider the words in the hymn "O Sacred Head Now Wounded": "What language shall I borrow to thank thee, dearest friend . . . ?" All six terms (*sacrifice, Messiah, penalty, gnostic intervention, logos, ransom*) became powerful symbols of what was experienced by those early Christians. They conscientiously used the language and thought forms of their day to proclaim the activity of God that they experienced in Jesus.

A Contemporary Metaphor

Those six metaphors are more or less helpful depending on one's life situation and the symbols that a person finds meaningful. I do not believe that any one of the metaphors is an absolute. All are human attempts to explain what was experienced. Is it possible for us to create metaphors for our day that are different from these classic expressions? I believe so. Here is one that I have found helpful for my own life. The diagrams on pages 9 and 11 are attempts to put into a graphic display what I have found to be experiential.

I begin with a circle to represent a human life. That life has a center which forms the meaning-giving focus of life. Beside the circle is a non-inclusive list of some of the important aspects of life. The x's in the circle represent these various values, which are placed in a varied relationship to

Unfortunate (Unsaved) Life

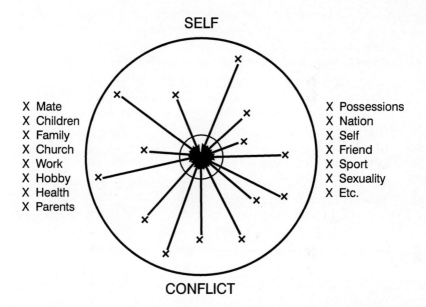

SELF

X Mate
X Children
X Family
X Church
X Work
X Hobby
X Health
X Parents

X Possessions
X Nation
X Self
X Friend
X Sport
X Sexuality
X Etc.

CONFLICT

If the center is a vacuum, the self is often game for any meaning giver or givers to rush in and fill the void. The result is conflict, with competing values attempting to possess the self.

Depending on one's state of life, the values will be closer to or farther away from the center.

the center. Parents, for instance, are close to the center in our childhood and are, in fact, in the center for most infants. As we grow older, our parents move out from proximity to the center. So with many other aspects of life.

If the center is a vacuum, any value can try to reach in and possess the center. (All this is speaking metaphorically, of course.) What we experience today is the state of conflict as various values vie to occupy that center. This is a state of conflict, or what H. Richard Niebuhr calls the "strife of the gods."[2] Who has not experienced the conflict between family and work? Or mate and some sport or hobby?

In the next diagram, on page 11, you discover love at the center. You are aware of being loved, or being accepted by that which is greater than you. From a center that knows love, a new possibility emerges. You can relate to all the other aspects of life at various distances from the center. Tensions can still occur between one value and another, but this is different from some value trying to invade the center and possess your very soul.

When we experience love at the center, this is a gift, the gift of the presence of God, who is the source of love. To say this another way: Jesus is the one who reveals to us that life can be lived in the midst of any circumstance with the confidence of eternal love being available. When we say that Jesus saves us, we are saying that Jesus gives us our identity as children of God. Jesus demonstrates that life can be lived with this kind of confidence. Jesus becomes the moral exemplar, the one we follow into the life of faith. As he called his disciples to "Follow me!" so he still calls. Many through the centuries have found salvation or wholeness of life in simply making the effort to follow the Man of Nazareth. This does not necessarily mean becoming an itinerant preacher living a single life. But at the least, it means living a life of love and compassion, responding to human need, forgiving the repentant, being open and relational with all kinds of people (regardless of nationality, race, sex,

A Contemporary Salvation Metaphor

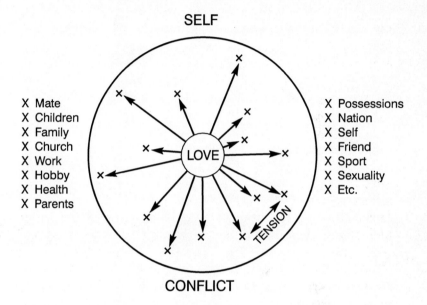

SELF

X Mate
X Children
X Family
X Church
X Work
X Hobby
X Health
X Parents

LOVE

TENSION

X Possessions
X Nation
X Self
X Friend
X Sport
X Sexuality
X Etc.

CONFLICT

If the self knows itself to be loved, absolutely and eternally, the center is occupied. From that center, each value can be related to, minimizing conflict.

Tensions may exist between one value and another, but not at the center, fighting for control. The assurance of love creates wholeness of life.

What does salvation mean? How does Jesus save us? By revealing the love of God and enabling us to accept that love! When we do so, we have the key to wholeness of life, which is nothing less than:

*Being absolutely related to the absolute and
relatively related to the relativities of life.*

class, or health). The mystery of the Christian Gospel is that the life of Jesus has empowered people through the centuries to love based upon the awareness that they are loved.

All this means that when we are absolutely related to the absolute, the love of God, we can be relatively related to the relativities of life. We are set free from absolutizing our mates, our children, our work, our pleasures, our health or any other aspect of life. At the same time we are set free to live lives of love and compassion. This is being saved or having wholeness of life. Is this good news? It is to me!

The Blending of Event and Story

One other subject is needed to understand some of what follows: the difference between event and story. The Christian Gospel is formed from two main elements: what happened in history, and how people interpreted what they experienced in history. The Gospel has fused together historical elements and the story language by which people gave testimony to the experience they had of God. These are hard to separate, but I have found it necessary to try in order to meet questioning minds, including my own. Many have doubts about what is presented at times as being historical. I offer the diagram on page 13 as a help to those who want to clarify the Christian Gospel.

Note first those elements in the life of Jesus that we can unequivocally call historical. Although some in the past have tried to make Jesus a mythological figure, the historical person is attested to by almost all scholars who have studied the material. Not only do we have the Gospel accounts, but references to the Man of Nazareth are made in Tacitus, a Roman historian; Suetonius, a biographer of the Caesars; and Josephus, a Jewish historian. What is listed on the bottom line are the elements in Jesus' life that have historical authenticity. Even the resurrection, which may be questioned as

Elements of the Christian Gospel

Event/Story

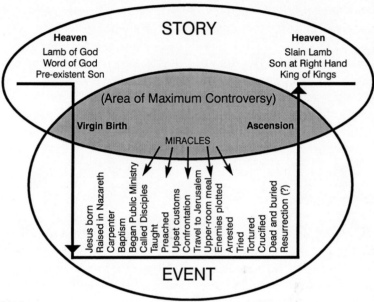

STORY

Heaven
Lamb of God
Word of God
Pre-existent Son

Heaven
Slain Lamb
Son at Right Hand
King of Kings

(Area of Maximum Controversy)

Virgin Birth   **Ascension**

MIRACLES

Jesus born
Raised in Nazareth
Carpenter
Baptism
Began Public Ministry
Called Disciples
Taught
Preached
Upset customs
Confrontation
Travel to Jerusalem
Upper-room meal
Enemies plotted
Arrested
Tried
Tortured
Crucified
Dead and buried
Resurrection (?)

EVENT

Notes:

1) The bottom line consists of events with some measure of historical credibility. Events are true if they happened.
2) The top two lines contain language that is not historical but symbolic or mythological. Such language is true if it describes in symbols what was experienced, i.e., is true to experience.
3) The language on top was used by the Christian community to interpret what they had experienced in relation to Jesus.
4) The virgin birth and ascension are transitional elements enabling the heaven dimension to come to earth and then return to heaven.
5) The miracles are between heaven and earth, with some Christians seeing them as events and others as stories.
6) The two big circles indicate what some see as event and others see as story, with the intersecting area in controversy.

to its nature, is a part of history that resulted in the radical change in the disciples and the birth of the Church.

On the top two lines, however, we have something else. What happened to those early followers of Jesus led them to express their experience with highly symbolic terms. *Lamb of God, Word of God, Pre-existent Son* can hardly be called historical language. Neither can we regard the Slain Lamb, Son Seated at the Right Hand, or King of Kings as other than mythological or symbolic in nature. Of one thing those early Christians were convinced: what happened in the life, death, and resurrection of Jesus was more than human activity. "God was in Christ reconciling the world to Himself. . . ." (2 Cor. 5:19) They had to use whatever language was available to make this testimony. The Jesus event had its origin in God, where God dwelt. Heaven was that transcendent realm, according to the thought-form of that day.

Those early communicators faced a problem. How did the heavenly dimension become earthly, and how did the earthly become heavenly? Two transitional movements became part of the Christian proclamation: the virgin birth and the ascension. We have labeled the historical material as event and the mythological terms as story. Are the virgin birth and ascension parts of the event or parts of the story? The arguments have persisted with no resolution. Add the miracle passages to these two transitional movements, and we discover what separates many Christians today. Did the miracles happen, or are they part of the story, testimonies to the power of Jesus to make changes in peoples lives? We use bodily conditions in symbolic ways today: "I was dead yesterday"; "I was deaf to her words"; "I was blind to what was going on"; "I was paralyzed and couldn't do a thing"; etc. Could not the Christian writers use these terms in like fashion? Or, more than that, could they not create stories to illustrate what they were experiencing? Some Christians see this possibility, and others do not.

Another problem emerges with the word *mythology.* For

many this raises a red flag. To say something is mythological says to many that it is not true. Not so! There are at least two kinds of truth. Scientific, provable truth forms a significant part of life today. Medical science and technology depend on accurate facts, provable data. We depend on this kind of truth. But another form of truth is more personal and existential. Shakespeare was in touch with this truth in a quote, as evidenced in a quote from *As You Like It:*

> And this our life, exempt from public haunt,
> Finds tongues in trees, books in the running brooks,
> Sermons in stones, and good in everything. (II.1)

One interested in facts could change this to conform to provable truth and suggest that it should read:

> Finds trunks in trees, sermons in books,
> Stones in the running brooks . . .

This would be factual but would miss the profound personal truth that anyone in tune with nature can recognize in the original.

Another, more personal, example will illustrate my point. While courting my wife, who was in Scarritt College in Nashville when I was in SMU in Dallas, I sent her a German love poem that I discovered in studying German poetry. She would have to get it translated—a college prank. Here it is:

Du bist mein, ich bin dein,	You are mine, I am yours,
Des sollst du gewiss sein.	Such will it ever be.
Du bist verschlossen	You are locked up
In meinem Herzen,	In my heart.
Verloren ist das Schlusselein:	Lost is the key:
Du must immer drinnen sein.	You must ever remain there.

Is this true? Locked up in my heart? The key gone? Factually, this is nonsense. But is this true to my understanding of the relationship between my wife, Frances, and me? Yes, personally and meaningfully true! This is the kind of experiential truth that plays a more important role in the Bible than factual truth. To say that some portion of the Scriptures is story is, therefore, not saying that it is untrue. The story may be more true to experience than any historical fact.

Now, with this background, we are ready to move on to the chapters. Each chapter begins with a statement of what does not have to be believed and is followed with what many believe about what they do not believe. Obviously, there are those who do believe the initial statements in spite of all the evidence to the contrary. I am merely asserting that you do not have to. While some Christians are uncomfortable without certainty in believing and experience tension because of unanswered questions, others are challenged to explore the value of non-traditional expressions of the faith. This book is not designed to give absolute answers but to provoke thinking on matters of faith and life and to point to truths that are more profound than literal statements. My hope is that this will contribute to the faith journeys of those willing and eager to question what are the experiential truths found behind the faith statements of the past.

Be patient toward all that is unresolved in your heart. And try to love the questions themselves. Do not seek out answers that cannot be given you, because you would not be able to live them, and the point is to live everything! Live the questions now. Perhaps you will then gradually, without noticing it, live along some distant day into the answer.

—Rainer Maria Rilke

– 1 –

The Bible as the Word of God

A Christian does not have to believe that the Bible contains the literal words of God.

But Christians can believe that the Bible becomes the word of God as time and again it enters into dialogue with us, leading us to significant insights and/or profound changes in our lives.

If we were to ask any Christian group, "What is the Bible?" the response would be a chorus: "The Word of God." That is the traditional phrase that we have heard all through our years. However, unless one can answer the second question, the first is almost meaningless. The second question is simply: "What does that mean?" Either the response is just silence, or we listen while people flounder in their effort to respond. What are some responses to that second query?

A few might say that the Bible was given to us by God,

and every word is his so that God can be quoted. Such a response is a bit hasty. The Bible was not handed down from heaven. The formation of the biblical canon (authoritative books) took about 1,000 years from the discovery of the book of Deuteronomy in the Hebrew Temple in 621 B.C.E. to the acceptance of the sixty-six books by Christians in the middle of the fourth century. Whatever biblical inspiration means, it certainly does not mean that this book was given to us in one fell swoop.

Neither is the Bible divine dictation with the authors acting as secretaries. A secretary types a letter, recorded or dictated by another. The content reflects the other's ideas, character, and purposes. When we read the Bible we can readily see that the distinctive characteristics of the human authors are evident in their writings. For example, Amos is quite different from Hosea. Amos uses a clever technique to get his message across to the people of Israel. He speaks first about the sins of the neighboring countries, all of whom were regarded with suspicion by the northern kingdom. After he has his hearers agreeing with him, he "lowers the boom." Now, for you in Israel! Hosea speaks in a different vein. He is called by some the weeping prophet. He identifies with the evils he sees about him and agonizes over the word that he is led to speak. Each author is present in the words spoken and written.

The Gospel writers are each unique with emphases determined by the authors' own purposes and faith perspective. Mark presents Jesus as the activist doer and the disciples as uncomprehending dullards most of the time. Matthew writes about Jesus as the Jewish rabbi or teacher and places the disciples in a more sympathetic light. Luke paints a word picture of Jesus as a great storyteller and includes the most famous of his parables. John writes of Jesus as the philosopher who combines the Hebrew wisdom tradition with Greek philosophical concerns; John has many long philosophical discourses. Paul is proud of his

Pharisaical training, convinced that he had the right to be an apostle, angry at times with the misinterpretation of his message by some of the churches he founded. At the close of more than one letter he wrote: "See with what large letters I write with my own hand!" Perhaps Paul had an eyesight problem and dictated his letters but decided to add this personal note.

The writers of the Bible were not taking words dictated to them by God. They were God-conscious people, under conviction, communicating what they perceived to be the message of God to a specific situation. The prophet addressed the people with the word: "Thus says the Lord." This was the mark of the prophet who dared to believe that he was speaking for the Lord. The word *prophet* means speaking on behalf of another. The prophet was a spokesperson for the Divine as he was able to understand the mind of God. Were the prophets always right? No, but that is another story.

The Word of God, as the Bible is often called, does not refer to the words but to the creative wisdom of God that is active in human life and disclosed in the biblical message. *Word* is the translation of the Greek *logos*, which means the divine, creative wisdom that brought the universe into being. (See Salvation Metaphors diagram on page 4.) John writes that the Word was made flesh and dwelt among us. This is one of the proclamations that has stood the test of time. It is a testimony of the divine wisdom that was and is experienced in the life and death of Jesus. That Word is a dialogical and confrontive word that time and again has addressed people in a personal way. More accurately we can say that the Bible becomes the Word of God as we are addressed and our lives are called into question.

Christians from the fundamentalist right wing of Christendom insist on the Bible's inerrancy and infallibility. This perspective assumes that security is found in absolutizing the Bible produced by first-century Christians, instead of the God revealed in the events and stories of that period of history. Fundamentalists take the Bible and literalize all the non-poetic passages in the Bible, with the possible exception of the dietary laws and holiness code of the Jewish scripture. They assume that the passage "All scripture is inspired by God" (2 Tim. 3:16) means the Bible as we know it. But scripture at the time 2 Timothy was written was simply the Jewish Law and the Prophets. The Bible that we know was not formed until the fourth century. More than that, "inspired by God" did not make the scriptures absolute or inerrant. It was not so for Jesus, who said, "They said of old . . . but I say to you . . . ."

Even the earliest days were marked with a variety of ways of interpreting the sacred writings. The allegorical or symbolic method was used by early Church fathers following after the Jewish philosopher Philo Judeus, who so interpreted the Jewish Scriptures. To jump past the Dark and Middle Ages, when the Bible was entrusted to the Church elite, to the Renaissance/Reformation period, we find a new excitement about Bible study; but in spite of words to the contrary, the Bible was not absolutized. Luther called James an epistle of straw and wanted to put Revelation in a second canon. And Calvin, who certainly had a high view of the Bible, was able to say that Mark was wrong about a matter. Calvin also called the early Genesis stories *balbutive,* meaning "baby talk." The stories were designed for simple minds and were not to be taken literally. Karen Armstrong, in her mind-expanding book *The History of God,* brought this to my attention. Wesley in the eighteenth century expressed the desire to be a man of one book, *sola scriptura,* and yet was a man of many books, taking the Bible as a primary but not exclusive authority. Wesley insisted that the Bible be interrelated with tradition, experience, and reason. None of these men equated the words of the Bible with the literal words of God.

Where, then, did fundamentalism, biblical literalism, get its ideology? Not from the first century; not from the

Church fathers; not from Luther, Calvin, or Wesley. Some see the birth of modern fundamentalism in a Church event which occurred in 1870: the promulgation of the doctrine of the Infallibility of the Pope. The Roman Catholics had an infallible voice. Where is infallibility for Protestants? Little by little, some elements of Protestantism began to assert a paper Pope, the infallible Bible. As far as we know, the first use of the word *inerrancy* for the Bible was by Archibald Hodge shortly after 1870. Near the same time, Benjamin Warfield brought into usage the term *infallibility* in reference to the Bible.

The Bible is the textbook of the Christian faith, but this does not mean that we must view the Bible as the literal words of God. The Bible contains many types of literature depending on the thoughts, desires, and inclinations of the authors. A survey of its pages reveals poetry, drama, short story, essay, history, fable, letter, parable, allegory, mythology, and apocalyptic writing—to name some. To ask proper questions of written material, we need to have some idea of what we are reading. Asking historical or scientific questions about that which is not history or science produces nonsense answers. To miss the allegorical nature of Jonah, for instance, leads to questions about the size of a large fish's gullet and the amount of oxygen to be found in a whale's stomach. Such questions miss the whole purpose of the book.

All this means that the Bible is a rich source of inspirational material. In its pages we find the distillation of wisdom from the ancient past. Our roots are in this book and in the people whose story is told in this book. We do not have to see the Bible as God's literal words for the Bible to speak to us today. Better to see the Bible as a book of human words that become the Word of God as here and there, now and then, we are confronted and God speaks to us through the biblical message. At least that is what this Christian and many others believe about what we do not believe.

– 2 –

Adam and Eve

A Christian does not have to believe that Adam and Eve were historically the first two humans and that creation occurred in six days or even six thousand years.

But Christians can believe that Adam and Eve are symbolic figures, representing every man and woman, and that the creation story affirms that behind creation is purpose, plan, and love.

The creation stories present problems to the modern mind. Many toss them out of consciousness in deference to the scientific mind-set of our time. Many Christians remain ignorant of the fact that all but a small minority of Bible scholars regard the creation stories as other than history or science.

What kind of literature are the creation stories in Genesis? No chronicler was present to record the beginnings of the natural world. Therefore, these stories cannot be history. Science as we know it was unknown when Genesis was written. These stories cannot be science. What are these stories, then? They fit the category of mythology, but many persons are uncomfortable with this word because they think it means untrue. Not necessarily so. Mythology is pre-historical or non-historical writing that expresses the understanding of a people in thought form and imagery emerging over a long period of time. Joseph Campbell, in his lifetime of work on mythology, has revealed the connecting mythological ties of ancient cultures. The TV series on PBS a few years ago featuring Bill Moyers' interviews of Campbell, and the book *The Power of Myth,* an elaboration of that series,[3] have shown how meaningful myth is in illuminating the human situation. Science can take us only so far; its truth is relative to the factual information available at any given time. Mythology probes deeply into human consciousness to reveal those primal elements that unite the human family. Because of that, mythology is at a different level of truth.

Genesis, as mythological writing, is *more* true instead of less true, because it is sensitive to the personal and social dimensions of human experience. The creation stories, when equated with historical or scientific fact, make no rational sense; but as symbol and metaphor, these stories express profound truths. Mythology has developed in all cultures. As a great storyteller has said, "All stories are true. Some of them happened." One truth is factual; the other is mythological.

When dealing with the creation stories, the basic questions to ask concern not what and how, but who and why. Not did it happen this way, but what does the story mean? For our purposes we are not considering the story of creation in Genesis 1-2:4a, which is the later in time of the two stories in the Bible. This story came out of Babylonian captivity and was designed to help preserve the sacredness of the Sabbath day. This narrative has humanity as the pinnacle of the creative process. The other, older story beginning in Genesis 2:4b reflects the work of a theologian who, for lack of a better name, has been designated J because of the word he used for God. This story places human beings at the center of a circle, the animals created after humans, not before as in the first chapter. The ancient Hebrew apparently was not very concerned that these stories did not agree. The purpose of the story was not descriptive science but a more profound truth. The Bible is a window. Some stare at the window and analyze what they see. Others look through the window to see what is on the other side. We here are doing the latter.

Following the story of the creation of the androgynous man and the wrenching of the female out of him, when the human's loneliness was not assuaged by the animals, we see the differentiation of the sexes. Yes, the story is told from a patriarchal worldview. We could tell it the other way. Man is created for woman. Each is made for the other. The male/female polarity is present in life. We see it in the sexes, and we see it within our individual lives. Maleness and femaleness are present in each of us. We are attracted to the other, because the other represents the undeveloped part of our own nature. The story tells us something about our incompleteness.

Now the narrative takes another turn. The man and woman are in the garden, caring for it with only the restriction not to eat of that one tree. That tree is the symbol of the difference between the human creature and God. God is the creator, and humans are the dependent creatures. Obedience is a product of dependency. We are to live in the garden on God's terms and not our own. God sets the boundaries and the rules. We cannot know what God knows.

The tempter comes in the form of a snake. What does one do with a talking snake? Nothing, if this is recognized as a fable, a part of the mythology or story. The snake speaking is no more a surprise to Eve than was Balaam's ass speaking to Balaam in Numbers 22:28 ff. These are two fables involving talking animals. We are dealing here with story and not event. The snake asks, "Did God say that you are not to eat of any tree in the garden?"

Eve responds, "We can eat the fruit of all but that one tree. We cannot eat or touch that fruit or we shall die."

"No, you won't," asserts the snake. "God knows that if you eat the fruit you will be like God." The tempter strikes at human weakness—the desire to be God, creator, and not creature. Eve saw the food, and it looked good. She had a gastronomic awareness. Eve noted that the fruit was a delight to the eye. She had aesthetic sensitivity. Eve also desired the fruit to make her wise. She longed for something more: for the spiritual beyond human limitations. Eve is physically alert, sensitively aware, and spiritually eager. She exercises discrimination and critical judgment, even though in the story she makes the mistake of trusting the snake. The man does not argue and capitulates quickly with the words "and he ate." And some interpret the Genesis story as asserting male dominance and supremacy?

Disobedience is the theme, the human desire not to be a limited creature but to be God. Milton said it: "Of man's first disobedience, and the fruit of that forbidden tree whose mortal taste brought death into our world and all our woe." (*Paradise Lost* I.1–3) This "first disobedience" is not speaking historically but existentially. The story is our story, yours and mine. This is our desire to be in control, to have certainty, to know without question.

The story follows with the couple hiding and being confronted. "Did you eat of the fruit?" the question is put to Adam. "The woman gave it to me," he blurts out. Their togetherness in disobedience did not unite but separated them. "What have you done?" is God's question to Eve. "The serpent beguiled me and I ate." Here is the first story of the passing of the buck, and it has been going on ever since. The story continues with the man naming the woman Eve, a word related to the Hebrew term for "living." God then orders them out of the garden. Then an amazing thing happens. Before they go, God makes for them comfortable garments of skin. God cares for them even as He sends them out into a world of suffering and pain. Now they are outside of Eden, which means that is where we are.

This is our story. An inspired author in the long ago has written the story of our lives. He might have written it another way, but this is what he did, and he has expressed some of the deepest truths of human life. We are dependent; we are not God. We have been created to live in relationship with one another. Though at times we do not like to be dependent and try to be lord of our own lives or the lives of others, we discover judgment in one form or another. When I choose my own way in an attempt to live free and unrestricted, I become a rebel and fugitive. I try to hide. The judgment comes, but God's judgment is not vindictive. God cares and provides for me the comforts of life, even as I struggle with life.

We live outside of the garden of perfection in a violent world, a world filled with agony and struggle. Only the very young are innocent. With every new birth we see a small Eden that does not last. Every newborn expects good from all. We lose innocence inevitably, but we are aware, sometimes unconsciously, of another world over against this world of struggle. In this other world, all is right. Perhaps we can capture it again. This is the purpose and plan of the originator. There is nothing for us to go back to; but perhaps here and there, now and then, we can bring that world into this one. We are not alone in the struggle. In revelatory moments, we are aware of the One who provides the garments of comfort for us and others. In this awareness, we are drawn to one another and to God by our suffering.

Outside of Eden we discover a new possibility to be related in faith. This is not a Godforsaken world. God is with us. Speaking symbolically, God has become flesh and meets us in the Adams and Eves of our world. Even as God was in the Suffering One, God still is in the suffering ones of our day. A new tree is offered to us: "I am the vine (tree), you are the branches." (John 15:5) We are nurtured by the tree of life, even as Adam and Eve were nurtured and cared for in the biblical story.

Christians do not have to believe that Adam and Eve were historical persons. We can join the majority of biblical scholars and believe that they are symbolic figures representing you and me, every man and woman. The story tells us truthfully about our creaturely state, our dependence, our desire for community (man and woman forming the first community), our desire to be God, our rebellion, God's judgment, and God's love in spite of human failings. In the words of the hymn writer Fred Pratt Green: ". . . for the wonders that astound us, for the truths that still confound us, most of all, that love has found us, thanks be to God."[4] The truth of Adam and Eve and the whole creation story does not depend on the account being history. At least that is what this and many other Christians believe about what they do not believe.

– 3 –

God Speaking

A Christian does not have to believe that God at one time spoke audible words to Abraham, Moses, Elijah, or any others.

But Christians can believe that biblical conversations with God represent that inner dialogue between the individuals and the divine will.

One does not have to believe as historical and factual all the stories in the Bible. Their truth is not dependent on actual happenings. A truth deeper than fact is often hidden behind what is written. A core of historical fact is certainly part of the patriarchal narratives as well as the accounts of the judges, kings, and prophets, but the creativity and inspiration of the authors move beyond mere fact. The Bible is more, not less, significant and meaningful because of this. This leads us to the statements above.

A Christian does not have to believe that God at one

time spoke audible words to any biblical characters. These intimate manifestations of God to human beings at definite times and places are called *theophanies*. Such theophanies are present in the *Iliad* of Homer as well as in Genesis, where God walked in the garden and spoke directly to Adam and Eve. Later writers tended to spiritualize such accounts as Moses and the burning bush and on Sinai, Elijah at Mt. Horeb, and Jesus at his baptism and transfiguration. The fact that such theophanies often appear as historical and that later people treated them as such does not make them so. In the West we are not often aware that the East does not tend to separate the subjective and objective worlds as neatly as we do. People in the East often accept as true the meaning of stories without raising the issue of facticity. This was especially true in the past and is true to a large extent today.

Somewhere Harry Emerson Fosdick tells the story of a group he led on a trip to Palestine. One morning they decided to have a devotional under an especially beautiful tree near the hotel where they were staying. Before they began their service, an official from the hotel came up to them requesting that they move somewhere else. He explained that the tree was regarded as holy by some of the people in the area. They did move and proceeded with their service. Several days later they were in another village and heard a strange story about their devotional service. The word had spread that these Americans had tried to speak under the holy tree but the spirit of the tree took away their voices. They were unable to speak as long as they remained under the tree. When they moved, their speech returned. The facts were all true; the explanation was a blend of the facts and the local people's subjective interpretation of the facts.

A Christian does not have to believe that God spoke audible words to any biblical characters. Many regard the biblical conversations with God as inner dialogues between the individuals and the divine will as that will was understood.

The accounts were written many years—in some cases, hundreds of years—after the supposed incidents. The stories reflected the theological understanding of a later age. The truth of such accounts is in the subjective and not the objective dimension of life.

Literalists, of course, have problems with this point of view. In the last century, some Christians, disturbed about the emerging historical-critical approach to the Scriptures, sought to explain the phenomena of biblical theophanies and why God was not speaking now. Out of this concern, dispensationalism was proposed as the answer to such questions. The dispensationalists claimed that God had tried, through the centuries, various methods of reestablishing the relationship with humans. As each was unsuccessful, God abandoned the method before trying another. According to the adherents of this viewpoint, all history is divided into dispensations. How God operates in one is different from how He functions in another. The Schofield Bible is a product of this kind of thinking.

Perhaps the subject will be clearer if we examine two of the many theophanies and note the theological issues involved. First read the story in Exodus 3 of God's call to Moses to return to Egypt and free the Hebrew people. Note especially Moses' desire to know God's name before he agrees to the task. The name had to do with the nature and character of the one named. The Hebrews came to be a people who were never to speak God's name. The name was spoken only by the high priest in the Holy of Holies on the Day of Atonement. Substitute names were used in place of the personal name. For example, God could be called Adonai, Elohim, or El Shaddai, but Yahweh (we think) was not to be spoken. The theophany reflects a much later period of history attempting to justify the restrictions on the use of God's name. Whatever the rootage in the life of Moses, scholars are in general agreement that this narrative comes from a more sophisticated age than the time of Moses.

Still more than the sacredness of the name is involved. To name is also to control. To be able to use a name is to have a measure of control over the one named. Some time ago I had a jogging route that took me by a house with a rather vicious dog that gave every appearance of wanting to bite me in the leg. I did a backward run until I moved out of his neighborhood. Each day I ran, the same confrontation occurred until one day I found the owner of the dog in the yard and urged her to call the dog home. She cried out, "Pepper, come!" The next day that I ran, Pepper came after me as before, but this time I called out, "Pepper, no!" Pepper very obediently turned around and went home. With Pepper's name, I had assumed a measure of control.

The Hebrew concept of the sovereignty of God meant that God was not subject to human control. God's name, therefore, was sacred and not to be spoken. Whenever others asked about their God, they did not point to a statue or name a name. They simply told their story. If they used "Adonai," they were not using the name of God but pointing to a relationship. That is why Adonai is translated "Lord" in the English Bible. *Lord* is not God's name but indicates our relationship to God. God is master, and we are servants. Concern about the name of God represents later thinking. This means that we do not have to believe in the literal conversation between God and Moses.

Or examine another theophany, from a later period. In 1 Kings 7, the story is told of Elijah, who had fled in fear from the queen Jezebel after his confrontation with the priests of Baal. The Word of the Lord came to him, but what was this Word? Some want to believe that these were spoken words. Others believe that the Word was more of a subjective experience than an objective one. Was Elijah's experience an objective confrontation with God, or a subjective "hearing" of the questioning of God: "What are you doing here, Elijah?" Whatever the experience, the result was that Elijah went back to complete his duties.

The Middle East and Orient have had their gifted story-tellers. Their stories move deeper than facts and probe into the subjective experiences of the major characters. The Eastern world did not, and does not now, separate subjective and objective as neatly as we do in the West. Their stories are true at a deeper level than a mere relating of facts. The fusion of subjective and objective, together with the story-telling nature of the world of that day, gives us another perspective on theophanies. I suspect that a poetic mind-set comes closer to seeing the truth than a literal one. Consider the words of Elizabeth Barrett Browning:

> Earth's crammed with heaven,
> And every common bush afire with God;
> But only he who sees takes off his shoes—
> The rest sit round it and pluck blackberries.
> *Aurora Leigh,* Book VII

Plucking blackberries could be construed as being so involved with making everything literal that deeper meanings are missed. But there are those who are open to see and hear the presence of God in the world about us. God is in everything and everything is in God. Some Christians may want to believe in God's speaking to people in that day, but a Christian does not have to believe that God actually spoke audible words. There are other explanations for the theophanies in the Bible that probe deeply into the human psyche to the subjective aspects of life. At least this is what many Christians believe about what they do not believe.

– 4 –

The Miracles of Moses

A Christian does not have to believe that at Moses' decree the Nile turned to blood and various calamities afflicted Egypt, contravening the laws of nature.

But Christians can believe that the Moses stories point to a remarkable figure in history and assert his powerful influence.

Many Christians are intent on affirming the facticity of much that was intended to be symbol and story. They are, of course, free to do this. Such intent, however, is often at the expense of the meaning and significance of the passages in question. The conviction seems to be that believing the unbelievable is an act of faith that has some merit with God, assuring them of being faithful believers. The result has been an anti-intellectualism and an obscurantism that hide the basic truths of the biblical message. Such believing has

35

no material effect upon the active life of faith. This is certainly true about the stories of Moses.

A Christian does not have to believe that the miracles attributed to Moses are historical accounts. Some may accept these stories as factual, but their doing so is contrary to both modern experiences and contemporary understandings of the natural order. But believing or not believing such stories is not essential for faith. Many are aware that the ancient world often surrounded significant leaders with a mythos that testified to that person's powerful influence. The Elijah and Elisha narratives in the two books called Kings in the Hebrew Scriptures are of a like nature. Moses is a pivotal figure in Hebrew history, called the founder of Hebrew religion. The amazing thing is not the miraculous stories but the truth that both Jews and Christians have found by not looking at but through these stories.

What is behind the Hebrew Exodus? The Hebrews lived for several hundred years in Egypt with relative freedom. Joseph, the son of Jacob, held a high position given him by the Egyptian king. The story of Joseph is a fascinating one involving, among other things, his ability to interpret dreams. He was a Jungian before Jung, or so it seems. In any case, the book of Exodus tells us that "there came a new king over Egypt, who did not know Joseph." (Ex. 1:8) The new king was disturbed by this foreign element in his nation and enslaved them lest they unite with some invader. The Hebrews became slave laborers for Egyptian building programs. When they continued to multiply, according to the Exodus story, the king ordered male infants to be killed to prevent the Hebrews from multiplying. Moses was hidden by his mother, later placed in the reeds by the river, adopted by the princess, nursed by his mother, and then raised in the king's household. As an adult, Moses killed an Egyptian who was beating a Hebrew. He fled for his life to the land of Midian. There he married and had a son. He worked for his father-in-law Jethro as a sheepherder. We have already mentioned the theophany in the previous chapter. Suffice it to say that Moses returned to Egypt and is credited with leading the Hebrews out of slavery. The process involved a series of miracles disrupting Egyptian life that finally persuaded the king to let the Hebrews go. The miracles began with a rod being changed to a serpent, the Nile River turning to blood, a plague of frogs, insects, death of livestock, boils, hail, locusts, and the final calamity—the death of the first-born.

What a tremendous story! What do we make of all this? Is this history, and are we looking at a factual account? Or is this legendary material testifying to the significance of Moses as the father of Jewish religion? Christians and Jews differ in their responses to such questions. At the same time, can we not say that the truth of the Exodus is not dependent on the miracles of Moses? Many assert that they are a part of the hyperbole so characteristic of the East. Their storytelling involves employing excesses to make a point. We do not have to think that the heroes of Jewish history were treated differently than heroes in other traditions.

Therefore, a Christian does not have to believe in the miracles of Moses as history to understand the truth of the Exodus. Which leads us to the question: What is that truth? The Exodus story gives us a paradigm, a pattern for the way life is. Here it is:

> Slavery
> Freedom
> Wandering in the Wilderness
> Arriving in the Promised Land
> Another Slavery

This is the history of the Jews. Isaiah uses this Exodus paradigm when the Hebrews were in slavery later in Babylonia. In Isaiah 40, instead of the Red Sea, the obstacles to their return home were the mountains and the desert.

Isaiah proclaims that God is going to act in an Exodus way again. "Every valley shall be lifted up, and every mountain and hill be made low; the uneven ground shall become level, and the rough places a plain. And the glory of the Lord shall be revealed, and all flesh shall see it together, for the mouth of the Lord has spoken." (Is. 40:4–5) The mouth of the Lord was Isaiah, the prophet. Was Isaiah using the Exodus story in a literal fashion? It does not seem so. Was Isaiah in touch with the meaning of the Exodus? Most assuredly this was the case.

The New Testament tells the Jesus story using Exodus themes. Consider the Gospel of Mark. Jesus goes down into the water and comes out of the water (like the Red Sea). What does he do then? He goes into the wilderness for forty days, which would remind any Hebrew listening or reading of the forty years wandering in the wilderness. The Hebrews are tempted; Jesus is tempted. Later Jesus feeds the five thousand even as the Hebrews were fed by manna in the wilderness. Jesus also drove out the demons from a man whose name was Legion (Roman legions, Egyptian chariots?). The demons went into a herd of swine who rushed headlong into the sea and were drowned, just as the pursuing Egyptians were drowned in the Red Sea. Is all this accidental? Or is this telling of the Jesus story using Exodus themes to say that God in Jesus is acting in an Exodus way to set people free? The Exodus has become the *locus classicus* for both the Hebrew and Christian understanding of God's action.

This means that a Christian does not have to believe in the miracles of Moses to understand the truth of the Exodus. God still acts in an Exodus way. There is One who does not want to have people enslaved to anything. Consider the most obvious Exodus paradigm: drug or alcohol addiction. The slavery is the addiction. The freedom is a gift through therapy or with faith and will power. After the freedom is the agonizing wandering in the midst of constant temptation until the person arrives at the Promised Land. In time, some other addiction brings slavery again.

An addiction is having one's soul possessed (as represented in the diagram on page 9). An addiction is in fact a slavery. We get addicted to or enslaved by anything that is not absolute. Some get addicted to a person, for love can be an addiction. Many in our day get enslaved by their work. Others get addicted to a sport or hobby. The possible addictions or slaveries are legion. But there is One who does not want us enslaved to anything and who is the presence that disturbs us in our addictions and wants to set us free.

The Exodus paradigm is not dependent on believing literally everything in the Exodus story. Many Christians and Jews believe that God, through Moses, led the Hebrews out of Egypt but do not at the same time accept the miraculous details as factual. Are we less Christian or Jewish because of what our minds are unwilling to accept? I do not think so. At least, this is what many believe about what they do not believe.

– 5 –

Angels

A Christian does not have to believe that angels were visible spiritual creatures who spoke audible words to Mary and Joseph or anyone else in the Bible.

But Christians can believe that angels are the messengers in life who offer both presence and supportive help that radically change life situations.

Many stories in the Bible are believed by some Christians to be historical events. Other Christians believe that all stories are true but only some of them happened. The storytelling culture of the East was never intended to deceive anyone. Stories are the way ancient cultures, and even some modern ones, speak the truth about life. Behind such stories are profound understandings of the human situation. So we have noted about Adam and Eve and the

Moses narratives. Christians do not have to believe all stories as actual happenings, even though some may do so.

Christians do not have to believe that biblical stories
about angels are historical accounts meant to be taken literally. A few visionaries down through the centuries have
"seen" apparitions. Sensitive minds can conjure up visions
and images to meet specific needs. But angels serve a different function in stories. Where did the concept of angels
originate? A little excursion into angelology might be helpful in examining Christian beliefs.

Spiritual beings called angels came to us from Persian
religion, which passed through Judaism to Christianity.
They were developed as intermediaries between God and
humans. They could be friendly or hostile depending on the
desires of God or gods. They became agents for expressing
and revealing the will of the Divine. We find angels in the
Zend Avesta, the sacred book of Zoroastrians, and especially
the Gathas, which are seventeen hymns in the oldest part of
the Avesta. The Hebrews were tremendously influenced by
this religion while they were in Babylonian captivity.

Judaism developed a whole hierarchy of angels complete with four (or seven) archangels and myriad subordi-
nates. They were the servants and messengers of God. In
some Jewish Scripture they conveyed the mandates of God.
In other texts, angels were forerunners of special events. At
times angels were protectors of the faithful or dispensers of
judgment on adversaries. In the most familiar passages, angels stayed Abraham's hand, preventing the sacrifice of
Isaac; they reassured Jacob in his flight from his brother;
they escorted the Israelites through the wilderness; and
they fed Elijah in the desert. The story of Abraham enter-
taining angels unawares has its parallel in the classic tale of
Hynieus of Tanagra, who entertained three gods unawares.
In the Jacob saga, angels commuted by means of a ladder,
which is paralleled in Egyptian funerary texts and Greek poetry. Miniature ladders have been found in Egyptian graves.

These spiritual creatures appeared often at wells, at times beside oak or broom trees, and once at a burning bush, and they were the agents who troubled the waters at the effervescent spring at Bethzatha. (John 5:1-9) Such stories are well-known motifs from the folklore of other people, not only in Persian religion but also the Baal religion of the indigenous people the Hebrews met in what became Palestine.

How natural for the Christmas stories to have angels. These stories contain an angelic chorus and an angel speaking to the shepherds. The stories tell us about the birth of One who was to change radically the world. The early Christians thought that a transcendent reality must be behind such a life. The stories of angels announce that transcendent reference. Are angels in the event or story category? Many Christians are deeply moved by the Christmas stories without relegating them to history. The stories' truth is deeper than fact, which is also what many believe about the angels in the resurrection accounts.

As angelology developed, specific names were given to the archangels. The four most familiar are Gabriel, Michael, Raphael, and Uriel. The Pharisees believed in angels; the Sadducees did not. While the worship of angels was frowned upon by the early Church, a cult of angels developed in the fourth century, with Michael especially honored. Medieval Christian art is replete with angelic figures. Most Protestant leaders downplayed the place of angels. The Enlightenment period which followed relegated angels to the domain of poetic fancy and mythology.

What do we do with angels today? We do not have to believe in angels as literal beings. They can be regarded as symbols of spiritual forces. The word *angel* means "messenger," and messengers do come. Just as three men came to Abraham with a message and were called angels, so Jacob, disturbed by a guilty conscience, struggled with an angel at the river Jabbok. (The angel is the adversary variously called in the text "a man," "God," and later "an angel.") That angel, many of us believe, was a messenger from out of his own inner life. Jacob's guilt feelings, for having defrauded his brother and tricked his father, had been eating at him. Now that he was about to meet his brother again, Jacob was in inner turmoil. The story says that he wrestled all night with an angel. Others hold that the angel at the river Jabbok was part of primitive animism, the angel being the protector of the river. Jacob had to contend with the angel before he could cross. Personally, I prefer the first explanation.

We have all entertained angels unaware. The angels are the messengers whose presence and words make a difference in our lives. The angels who ministered to Jesus in the wilderness were the spiritual resources available to him. Some years ago, I was working on a sermon at our retreat cabin by Canyon Lake. The text was Jesus' temptations in the wilderness. I was struggling with what to do with the angels who the text says "came and ministered to him." On the way home to Austin, I was still troubled about my understanding of angels. Becoming a bit weary, I reached in the glove compartment for a tape and placed a Pavarotti recording in the cassette player. I did not know what was about to be played. Then I heard it: "Panis Angelicus"—Bread of Angels. I had a spiritual experience and almost stopped the car. An emotional surge almost overwhelmed me. My Latin being a bit rusty (the singing was in Latin), I tried to recall the English words. All that came to me was "and in temptation's hour," but that was enough. I said to myself: "Of course!" Where are you fed? What nurtures you? Jesus was not left alone to struggle with temptation, and I have not been alone, either. The messengers have been all about me through a lifetime. Angelic messages continue to emerge in human life to those who listen with the inner ear. The same angels that ministered to Jesus are available to us. In whatever form they take, the angels are the messengers of God. The angels in the form of parents, relatives, friends, authors, teachers, preachers, musicians, and others affirm (whether they know it or not) that God is present and active. God is not an absentee landlord. God is that positive pressure toward what is truly human, the force in history working for good. We do not have to believe in evanescent spiritual creatures. The stories about angels have meaning apart from any literalism. This is what many Christians believe about what they do not believe.

– 6 –

Virgin Birth

A Christian does not have to believe that Jesus was conceived as a biological miracle without a human father.

But Christians can believe that Jesus was unique and special, a one-of-a-kind representative of a higher dimension of life.

How strange that the virgin birth became an article of faith for some Christians! The conviction seems to be that believing the unbelievable is an act of faith that has some merit with God and assures believers of being faithful Christians. Mark, the earliest of the Gospels, makes no reference to the virgin birth. Paul, who wrote even earlier, either did not know the story or gave it no credence. If you believe that somehow God was uniquely in Jesus, what difference does it make how God got there? If you do not believe in this unique revelation, you have, of course, no problem. In either case, life is complex enough without trying to replace obstetrics with theology.[5] Instead, I would agree with the Hebrew tradition that sees God involved in every birth.

Where did the concept of virgin birth originate? We find it in many traditions. In Greek mythology, Dionysus became the god of wine. He was the son of Zeus, king of the gods, and Semele, the human and virgin daughter of king Cadmus of Thebes. When Dionysus was killed by the Titans, Zeus raised him from the dead to be immortal. The story of Romulus and Remus in Roman mythology has a similar theme. The twin boys were born to the war god, Mars, and the vestal virgin Rhea Silvia. After their birth, Rhea Silvia was buried alive for breaking her vows. The sons were placed in a basket and thrown into the Tiber River but were rescued by a she-wolf and later raised by a shepherd. Eventually their noble birth was discovered, and they helped their father-in-law regain his kingdom, of which he had been defrauded. Romulus and Remus decided to found a new city and went to the Tiber River, where they had been rescued. They became the founders of Rome in Roman mythology. Here are two virgin births. Consider one other culture. In the writings of Zoroaster, we discover that the world would have three saviors in a thousand-year sequence. Each one would be born of a virgin impregnated in a lake by the sperm of Zoroaster. Zoroastrianism greatly influenced Judaism and from Judaism found its way into Christianity.

Virgin births were part of the thought-forms of the Graeco-Roman world. It should come as no surprise, for those who know that ancient culture, that Christians relied upon the same ways of thinking to proclaim their faith in the uniqueness of Jesus. They affirmed One *"who was conceived by the Holy Spirit and born of the Virgin Mary."* For years this affirmation elicited little controversy. In our time, questions are being raised. Is this true? Born without a human father? Some say yes and attach faith here, insisting that this is a historical statement necessary for faith. Others say no, convinced that this is other than history.

This issue became focused at the turn of this century when a group of Christians produced a set of propositions called "Fundamentals of Christian Doctrine." Among them was one that affirmed the virgin birth as the primary witness to the deity of Jesus. The fundamentalist/modernist controversy over the virgin birth has waged long and loud ever since.

The Church of England formed a commission to study the virgin birth. It was to look at the proposition in relation to people's beliefs. The commission discovered that although many affirmed that belief in the "Word made flesh" is dependent on the belief in the virgin birth as a historical happening, others were convinced that belief in the incarnation is more consistent with the supposition that Jesus' birth took place under normal conditions of human generation. The commission came to the conclusion that both the views outlined were held by members of the Church, as well as members of the commission, who fully accepted the reality of our Lord's incarnation, which is the central truth of the Christian faith. The commission's report lifted the whole question out of the context of disputation. It faced honestly the fact of two schools of thought. It did not impugn the motives of one side or the other. It did not make the mistake of saying that to be a Christian one must believe one way or the other. The virgin birth may be an historical event, a literal happening, or it may be a wondrous tradition, the poetic expression of a profound faith. The basic issue, it seems to me, is not about believing the virgin birth literally, but whether the Christian faith should rest upon something so uncertain and so removed from our experience.

Yet, the virgin birth is essentially true in a depth dimension. As Frederick Buechner has written: "Whereas the villains of history can always be seen as the products of hered-

ity and environment, the saints always seem to arrive under
their own steam. Evil evolves. Holiness happens."[6] What is
true about the saints is pre-eminently true about Jesus. In
every person rests the mystery of specificity. Why this person, in this place, at this time? We affirmed that this mystery is heightened in Jesus. Why this man? In the place
where he was born? In that period of history? Christians affirm that the Holy Spirit was especially there. The meaning
of the Nativity stories is exactly at this point. Some
Christians choose to affirm this literally and physically.
Others believe that the Spirit operates through normal
processes. There is no real need for controversy. Let us not
divide the body of Christ over opinions. John Wesley, one of
our fathers in the faith, put it this way: "The Word was
made flesh. I believe this . . . . There is no mystery in it. But
as to the manner how he was made flesh, wherein the mystery lies, I know nothing about it; I believe nothing about it;
it is no more the object of my faith than it is of my understanding."[7]

Is it not possible for us to choose our interpretation and
at the same time not exclude from the Christian family
those who choose another? For both opinions, the birth stories are amazing parts of our tradition. They hold together
two affirmations: the divinity of Jesus, *"conceived by the Holy
Spirit,"* and the humanity, *"born of the Virgin Mary."* With this
latter phrase, the early Church was concerned not about divinity but about humanity. The Docetists were saying that
Jesus was not human, that he was a spirit assuming the appearance of flesh. The Creed, in contradiction, affirms that
he was born of a woman's body as we were. He was flesh
and blood.

What, then, do we do with the virgin birth? I am saying
that a Christian does not have to believe in this birth as a biological miracle, although many Christians do. On the other
hand, the affirmation does have a depth meaning. I prefer
to start with the known and move to the unknown. We

know something about the response to Jesus of the early Christians. We have experienced the God dimension in our own lives. Out of the experience of the past and my own experience, I affirm the presence of God in the midst of life. I know also that for me Jesus is at the center of this understanding. His divinity does not depend on a theory about the mode of his birth, but on what he has done for me and for humanity.

The virgin birth is important, not historically but theologically, not literally but spiritually. It is one of many testimonies to the significance of Jesus and to his uniqueness. This is what many Christians believe about what they do not have to believe.

– 7 –

The Miracles

A Christian does not have to believe that the miracles told about Jesus' life and death were historical happenings.

But Christians can believe that the followers of Jesus experienced transformation, empowerment, and new life and used bodily health symbols to express the radical changes experienced, and that they fervently believed that his death had cosmic significance.

Christians do not have to believe as historical facts the miracles in the Christian Scriptures. Of course, we were not there, and what happened in any specific case is not available evidence. Some choose to read all the biblical narratives as historical references with no recognition of a theologically motivated tradition. Many, however, do not look today for literal resurrections, dramatic healings, and radical changes to natural laws.

Look first at the miracles related to bodily health. Except for a few Christian sects and Christian Science, most Christians rely on the medical profession to do its best to keep us healthy. All Christians, however, seem to acknowledge that faith and positive thinking contribute to good health and produce at times miraculous results. Having said this, what is behind all the healing miracles in the Christian Scripture?

John Shelby Spong, in his book *Resurrection—Myth or Reality?*[8], examines the Gospel accounts in the light of the midrash tradition of the Hebrews. This tradition assumes that whatever is venerated in the present must be connected with a sacred moment in the past. So the parting of Jordan's waters by Joshua, Elijah, and Elisha were replications of the power of God working through Moses at the Red Sea. This midrash tradition is present also in the Christian Scriptures. The feeding of the five thousand could well be a reminder of the feeding of the Hebrews by Moses when they were wandering in the wilderness. The ascension of Jesus can be connected to the story of Elijah's ascension. (See a later chapter on this subject.) The story of Jesus raising the widow's son at Nain is a parallel to that of Elijah raising a widow's son, as told in the book of Kings. The miracle tradition can well be seen as the Christian effort to place Jesus in line with the Hebrew greats of the past. The basic question, then, is not whether these miracles happened, but what was there about Jesus that led the authors to place him in this tradition? In the story of Jesus we seem to have the retelling of ancient themes within the accounts of Jesus' life and ministry.

What can we believe about the healing accounts in the Gospels? People did experience transformation, empowerment, and new life. Bodily health is the symbol of such change. Have you not said, "I was dead yesterday," or "She didn't hear what he was saying," or "He was blind to what was going on," or "I was lame when it came to doing something"? We use health words metaphorically. Do we think that biblical writers could not do the same? Not only that, could they not reach back into the past and find those stories related to their experiences with Jesus? As mentioned earlier, remember that Eastern culture has not and does not as neatly differentiate between the objective and subjective dimensions of life as does the Western. This has given us problems in understanding one another. If we see the miracle tradition in the light of Hebrew midrash, we can see miracles not as part of history but as part of story, the subjective tying together of past and present into the activity of God in human history.

Perhaps two miracle stories will help to illustrate this point. The first, told in the three synoptic Gospels (and also mentioned on page 38), is about a man (Matthew—"two men") so filled with unclean spirits (demons) that he was constantly crying out and bruising himself with stones. (Matt. 8:28–32, Mark 5:1–13, Luke 8:26–33) When Jesus asked his name, he replied, "Legion." Legion was appropriate for the many tormenting spirits but also a word for the Roman legions or the Egyptians pursuing the Hebrews. A herd of swine nearby served as repositories for the "demons." They came out of the man and entered the swine. Then they dashed headlong down a steep bank into a lake and were drowned. Now, could any Jew hearing this story not think of those earlier demons in the form of Egyptian soldiers who went into the lake and were drowned? This is a typical midrash telling of a story to tie together the past and the present. By viewing it as story, and not history, we do not have to be unduly concerned about the inconsistencies in the accounts.

The second miracle story is about the healing of a man at the pool of Bethzatha. (John 5:1–9) This could well have harkened back to the story of the healing of Naaman the leper, who was healed after bathing in the river Jordan. (2 Kings 5:1–14) According to the miracle story, a man who had been ill for thirty-eight years was waiting by an effervescent spring that supposedly had curative powers, especially for those who got there first. Earlier people claimed that a god lived in the pool. The Hebrews, being monotheists, asserted that angels were in the pool. Jesus came upon the scene and asked the invalid: "Do you want to be healed?" The sick man answered him, "Sir, I have no one to put me into the pool when the water is troubled, and while I am going another steps down before me." Here was a complainer, a malcontent, blaming others for his lack of wholeness. He was the typical "poor me." Jesus gave him an absurdly simple command: "Rise, take up your pallet and walk." He did and was healed.

Why was this story told? To prove that Jesus was the Son of God? If so, the telling failed. He was killed! Most people did not believe then because of this or any other miracle, nor, I suspect, is anyone convinced now by such stories. Was the story told to show that the way to get healed is to listen to Jesus' command to be healed? Healing sects abound that place great emphasis on faith healing, and some illnesses do respond to positive thinking and faith. Yet, I feel certain that, for most of us, healing comes from a healthy way of life and appropriate medical attention when necessary.

This story is told for a more profound reason, probing into the recesses of our subjective selves. This happened to me some years ago. After serving a church for a number of years, I received a call from my district superintendent (in the United Methodist system, the intermediary to the bishop) about moving to another church. I asked him if I had a choice, and he assured me that I did. I responded by saying that I preferred to stay where I was. An hour later I received another call. This time the d.s. pushed by saying that they (the six d.s.'s and the bishop) were of the unanimous opinion that I should take this new appointment. Again I asked if I had a choice. He assured me that they would work with my decision. "My wife and I want to stay where we are." A little later another d.s. called to tell me that if I didn't take this appointment, I could forget being considered for anything else for the time being. I reaffirmed our decision. A few minutes later the bishop called and explained: "Nineteen moves depend upon your taking this appointment. Are you a member of the team or not?" We moved.

For the next few weeks (or was it months?) I was the malcontent and complained to my family and a few friends. I had decided some weeks before to preach on the lectionary (selected texts for the Church Year agreed upon by numerous denominations). On a given Sunday, John 5:1–9 was the Gospel lesson. I looked at the text a little askance. I was a bit troubled by miracle stories. Yet, I had resolved to preach from the lectionary and began to work on the text. In one session I was struck suddenly by a truth I had not seen before. I was the man at the pool of Bethzatha. He was complaining because no one would help to place him in the pool. I was complaining because they were placing me where I preferred not to be. My life would be good when I was appointed to a place that I determined was right for me. Jesus' word was a word directed to me: "Rise, take up your pallet [your life situation] and walk." The Bible had become the Word of God to me. I was confronted, addressed, and I changed. That Sunday I preached with tears in my eyes. Do I care if that story really happened? No, the Word of God is there for those who are ready to hear. For me, whether or not that healing is historical is incidental.

The healing miracles can be seen in the light of Christian midrash. More than that, other miracles can also be understood from this same perspective. Some Christians believe that all non-poetic, non-metaphorical, and non-parabolic biblical statements are factual. What, then, do we do with the Gospel of Matthew's word that at the crucifixion the day became as night (Mark and Luke also) but also asserts that the earth quaked and graves gave up their dead? (Matt.

27:51–52) Is this to be taken literally? Of course not! If such had occurred, would not Tacitus (Roman historian) or Josephus (Jewish historian) have reported such happenings? Or, is this part of the Christian midrash? In the stories of Joshua, he ordered the sun to stand still so that he could kill more of his enemies. (Joshua 10:12–14) In Jeremiah and Ezekiel we find the word about the bones of the dead being raised out of the graves. (Jeremiah 8:1; Ezekiel 37:12) This is hyperbole at its best.

What was Matthew trying to communicate with these hyperboles? The death of Jesus has cosmic significance. This was no private event in an insignificant part of the world. The crucifixion, as Christians saw it, was an event of universal importance. To proclaim this, Matthew told the story of the created order responding—darkness, earthquake, dead rising. Mark and Luke could include the darkness, but the earthquake and dead rising was perhaps too much hyperbole for them. Some may choose to place this in the literal category. I do not know why they do. The basic question, however, is not, Did these incidents happen? but, What do they mean? The meaning and significance are found in the story which proclaims the truth that this death has cosmic implications.

The interpretation of the miracles does separate Christians. We can see this most clearly in an analysis of the only miracle story found in all four of the Gospels: the feeding of the five thousand. This was mentioned previously, but since this must have been especially important to the early Christian community, we now give the story a closer look and note at least three possible interpretations in addition to the one on page 38.

Some Christians accept the miracles as historical happenings. They feel no need to understand and remain undisturbed in the simplicity of their faith. They simply accept that Jesus was the incarnate Son of God with special powers, which meant that he could circumvent natural laws.

Wind and waves would obey his will; supply and demand did not limit him; bodily ailments all gave in to his powers. That Jesus took five barley loaves and two pickled fish and distributed them to five thousand people so that the leftovers filled twelve baskets is no problem for those who just accept the story as given.

From this perspective the miracles were simply to demonstrate that he was the Son of God and by his powers would win people to himself. Because of the miracles they would accept his leadership and his teachings. That many people hold this position without doubting or questioning is a fact. That they have a right to such an opinion is obvious. That they have a place among the People of God is certainly true.

The one problem with this viewpoint has been its failure to explain why the miracles did not produce the results they were supposed to. Jesus was killed, and the disciples became a discouraged and disheartened lot. The miracles are not what brought or bring people now into relationship with Jesus.

Other Christians read or hear the miracles and their minds raise questions. They feel that they must understand and find no shame in doubting the historicity of the miracles. Many such Christians regard the miracles not as what happened but what happens. They are simple stories to demonstrate the always and forever operative power of Jesus to change lives. These Christians interpret the miracles as other than historical happenings.

To many of the questioners the feeding of the five thousand is a story about generosity and sharing. One interpretation presents the miracle in a rather fanciful way. Jesus, wanting some time alone with his disciples, takes a boat and goes across the Sea of Galilee for a rest from the crowds. However, the people, not to be dissuaded, travel some miles around the lake and appear before him. They had come from several nearby cities, having heard of this teacher/prophet from Nazareth. Would they have walked miles with no pro-

visions for their needs, no food or drink? But the hordes of
people with their caches of food were reluctant to eat; they
did not know about the others. One lad known by the disciples was willing to share his loaves (really cakes) and fishes,
and Jesus took them and blessed the boy's generosity. His
act so shamed the crowd that all took out their food and
shared a glorious picnic and had twelve baskets left over.

Many like this interpretation. It makes more rational
sense, and we do not have to suspend our scientific or rational mind-set. The miracle becomes the transformation of
those who had food so that they became willing to share.
But this explanation has its drawbacks, as well. This is a
rather fanciful and sentimental treatment that takes away
the mystery. Moreover, we cannot say that this is any more
true than the very literal interpretation.

Still another interpretation is to recognize the story-
telling nature of Oriental people and the way objective and
subjective dimensions of life are not neatly differentiated
(as mentioned previously). In the feeding story, the experience could well have been: Once I was hungry but now I've
been fed. In the story, objective hunger is used to express a
subjective experience.

People do have deep spiritual needs. We all yearn or
hunger for something more than material goods will satisfy.
We are longing to find fulfillment in life, wanting to be fed
deeply. And God does fill the hungry heart. What is all this
saying? Christians having been fed by the Christian community and the word of the gospel, and looking back at how
the disciples and others must have been fed by Jesus, told
this story and it became a standard. Some scholars tell us
that this story is a prototype of the Eucharist, Holy
Communion. The same elements are present in two of the
Gospels. Jesus broke the bread, looked up to heaven, and
distributed the food. Small bits of food are used to feed a
multitude, but the feeding is not physical but spiritual.

Jesus is the bread of life. He who feeds on him shall

never hunger, Literally? Of course not. Symbolically. What do we need? To be loved, to be accepted, to have a place in the heart of God. Do we? Yes, assuredly yes. The truth in the feeding of the five thousand is that Jesus meets our needs, fills our deepest hungers. We have been and are fed by his life, death, and continuing presence.

I have experienced this deep feeding in my own life. Years ago I was a lonely Air Force officer stationed in San Angelo. My home had been in upstate New York. My father had joined the Marines and my brother entered the Navy. I had not seen my mother in years. By the grace of God and the invitation of a fellow second lieutenant, I found love, acceptance, and a place in a Methodist Church. This Church of Jesus Christ fed me deeply. I have not been the same since. There I made a decision for Christ, was baptized, joined the Church, and decided for pastoral ministry. It was all one decision, the result of being fed.

This was not just a one-time experience. Years later, married and with three children, we had a problem on our hands. Who has not had children problems? I discovered that the meaning of my life was focused on success as a pastor, husband, and father. These were the meaning givers but all inadequate because they are all changing. In the midst of agonizing about one of our children, I listened to my own preaching: that Jesus Christ is Lord, that the love of God revealed by Jesus is the center and meaning giver of life. This reality seeks always to define my life. When accepted, this reality enabled me to let go of something over which I had no control. That good news that I am loved and accepted irrespective of children, mate, success, or anything else fed and still feeds me deeply. When I was fed in San Angelo, there were baskets of leftovers. Later, on numerous occasions, I have found that being fed did not exhaust the love-food that was available. That to me is the meaning of the miracle of the feeding of the five thousand.

Now, I cannot force you to accept one explanation over

the others. I can only say that Christians can differ about the miracles and still be brothers and sisters together in the faith. Did this miracle happen as is stated? I cannot say. Did Jesus use a boy's generosity to shame a crowd and teach a lesson? I do not know. Or is this story speaking about our deepest hunger and how Jesus meets that need? Perhaps! The miracle speaks to different people in different ways. Do not ignore it. Wherever you are in your thinking, let the story speak to you and be prepared to be blessed.

We cannot know much about the miracles, but we can see the possibility that Christian midrash and Oriental hyperbole were involved in these stories. As Christian literature developed over almost a hundred-year period, experiences in the lives of those early Christians were related to the faith stories of the past to give a continuity to the faith. Experiences in the present day can be enlightened by use of these same stories. This is their timelessness. Some Christians may be motivated to believe all the stories as history, but they do not have to. Others will prefer to see these as part of the story that expresses the meanings found in Jesus of Nazareth. For the latter, the miracles are Christian midrash to be regarded as mythology and symbol. This is what many Christians believe about what they do not have to believe.

− 8 −

The Blood of Jesus

A Christian does not have to believe that the shedding of Jesus' blood has some miraculous power in itself.

But Christians can believe that blood is a symbol of life and that Jesus' life has had a powerful influence upon the world.

Nowhere is the symbolic or non-literal aspect of much of Christian testimony more clear than in the powerful symbol for life: blood. Even minor bleeding has an awesome nature to it. To see our blood flowing out from a wound is deeply disturbing. Loren Eiseley (scientist, poet, and essayist) was aware of this when he recorded the experience of a man who fell on a sidewalk, causing blood to flow from a cut on his forehead. As he saw his ebbing substance, he did a surprising thing. Looking at his blood, he murmured in compassionate concern, "Oh, don't go. I'm sorry (for what) I've done (to) you." The injured man was addressing blood cells, phagocytes, platelets, and all the wondrous things that had been part of him and "were dying like beached fish on the hot pavement." He reported "[a] great wave of compassionate contrition, even adoration . . . a sensation of love on a cosmic scale."[9] What the injured one was experiencing was the wonder of blood as an inner galaxy and the mystery of life that is represented by blood.

The Hebrew people made full use of this mystery. The blood of the sacrificial lamb was sprinkled on the people to signify that they were united in a common life. Some early Christians used this sacrificial language to communicate to Jewish people. We read in the New Testament such statements as: "For Christ, our paschal lamb, has been sacrificed." (1 Cor. 5:7) We have been "sanctified by the Spirit . . . for sprinkling with his blood" (1 Peter 1:2); ". . . how much more shall the blood of Christ . . . purify your conscience . . ." (Hebrews 9:14); "Since . . . we are now justified by his blood . . ." (Rom. 5:9).

Have we been sprinkled with his blood? Of course not! Is there some miraculous power in his blood? Not so. Are we literally justified by his blood? Blood is a symbol of Jesus' life. What this means is that Christians have been made new by this life. They proclaimed this experiential fact by using language borrowed from the Jews. When in Hebrews we read that "without the shedding of blood there is no remission of sin," this is true to ancient Hebrew thinking but hardly relevant today unless you believe in magic and witchcraft. These are historically relative passages. What they did in their day, borrowing language of various cultures to express what they experienced in the life and death of Jesus, we must do for our time.

When we read such texts and sing some of the hymns of the Church that extoll the power of the blood, we must transvaluate the language and see the meaning behind the words. Jesus' blood is Jesus' life. Christians are united by this life, a life poured out for humanity, a life of involvement in humanity, which means entering the sufferings of our day. We cannot really help another unless we enter the other's life. One who suffers is not helped by aloofness. On the other hand, to be involved in a life of loneliness, despair, sickness, and pain is to risk experiencing the discomfort in our own hearts and even losing some of our peace of mind. Jesus entered the sufferings of his time. His followers are called to do the same.

We help to relieve suffering by identifying with it. I remember a ninety-year-old man whom I visited in the hospital. He had been regular in church attendance until the degeneration of old age caught up to him. He had to go to a rest home, and when he tried to crawl out of bed, he fell and broke his hip in three places. Because of his age, surgery was not advised. I paid a visit during this time of intense suffering and discomfort. When I left I made an effort to search out my own emotions. I became aware that I was angry, angry that a life spent in public school education should end in this way. At whom was the anger directed? I could not say God directly, for my concept of God would not allow me to believe that God willed this specific suffering. My anger was for the way life is, and the way life is certainly is permitted by God. Yes, in a way, I was angry at God. We have no answer to the why of such suffering except that we are dependent creatures, dependent on one another and finally dependent upon God. So it was with Jesus, and so it is with us. As we are affected by the life of Jesus, we become willing to be involved in the sufferings of others. In this involvement, community is born, and we become the body of Christ.

In classes I teach, I sometimes use an expanded name tag to get the group acquainted. Using 4x6 cards, I ask people to list in one corner three persons in their lives (most supportive, a model, most significant now). In another corner, they are to list three places where they have known peace and comfort. In a third corner they record the three most important decisions they have made to date. The fourth corner is reserved for hurts: one from a parent or parents, another from a friend or friends, and another resulting from circumstances over which they had no control. Small groups of three or four meet and are asked to share a corner of their choice. The groups re-form three or four times to repeat the procedure. What I have discovered is that the hurts are shared least, but where they are shared, a level of community is developed that is not as likely with the other corners. When we share our hurts, we open the possibility for others to do the same. Our hurts unite us together in a common humanity. We enter the hurts of others and in the process a measure of supportive help is provided.

The blood of Jesus represents his suffering, not just on the cross but in all the sufferings of his lifetime. He was estranged from his family, misunderstood by his followers, vilified by his enemies, and troubled by rejection; he agonized over a life that was about to be cut short and finally suffered pain and death. In so doing, he entered our suffering and identified with us. Does this make any difference? It does to me, and I have seen the power of his suffering in countless others.

We believe in the efficacy of Jesus' life of suffering and death without having to adopt the imagery of Jewish sacrifice or using the imagery of blood to express this truth. At least this is what many Christians believe about what they do not have to believe.

– 9 –

Jesus' Descent into Hell

A Christian does not have to believe that after he died Jesus went to hell to preach to the lost of the past.

But Christians can believe that those in the past are included in God's seeking love, and God's Christ activity is the same yesterday, today, and forever.

Christians believe and disbelieve many things; and they also differ from one another. One church's understanding of the biblical message will vary from another's. Absolutists claim that their interpretation is right. They even claim that their position is not an interpretation at all but just taking the Bible literally. They fail to see that the literalizing method is itself an interpretation.

So it is with the word that Jesus after the crucifixion "descended into hell" (Apostles' Creed), which is an adaptation of the passage from 1 Peter 3:18–19: ". . . being put to death in the flesh but made alive in the spirit; in which he preached to the spirits in prison . . ." Ephesians 4:9 also states: "(In saying, 'He ascended,' what does it mean but that he had also descended into the lower parts of the earth . . .)" The creedal word as well as the biblical passages give many people problems. Hell or Hades and the underworld are not concepts with which most people are comfortable.

What happens in our minds when we hear the word *hell*? Most of us picture the flames, devils, and pitchforks of the paintings and writings of the Middle Ages. God was seen in that period as judge, sentencing the wicked to a fiery inferno. In Michelangelo's *Last Judgment,* God sits on an elevated throne, separating human souls. Some are directed to a place of bliss, others to everlasting torment. We see some tumbling into tongues of fire.

There are many who can no longer accept hell as a literal place. The old idea of heaven being up and hell being down is out of keeping with twenty-first-century cosmology. We do not live in the three-story universe of the ancient world. (See Chapter 12.) However, we need the concept of hell, not as a place to be located but as a state of being. Hell is a reality about life, but in terms other than place. Hell is a symbol of radical separation from what we were intended to be. At various times in our lives we all experience such separation.

Since Jesus went no geographical place, what could the word about Jesus' descent into hell possibly mean then and now? Initially, the Church was struggling against those who affirmed that Jesus was not a human being but a spiritual creature who could not suffer and die. The Church's official position was that Jesus was born of Mary, a woman, which would make him human. And he really died. He went to Sheol, the abode of the dead in Hebrew thought. Christians were affirming that he did not just appear to die; he really died his death and went to that place conceived in that day as the abode of the dead.

A little later another concern developed. What about all those who lived before, who were, they believed, in that spiritual prison or hell (Sheol)? How was God's love revealed in Jesus to be offered to them? They chose a unique way of bringing them into the kingdom: Jesus "going" to the place of departed spirits. The descent into hell is not unique to the Christian Scriptures. The ancient Sumerian myth of the goddess Inanna has her descend to the netherworld (the place beneath the earth). Inanna instructed her messenger, Ninshubur, that if she did not return in three days to set up a hue and cry for her in the assembly of the gods. In the underworld, Inanna dies; she becomes a corpse. Later, she does rise from the dead by means of the "food of life" and "the water of life"; and the myth asserts, "When Inanna ascends from the nether world, Verily the dead hasten ahead of her." Note the elements in the Inanna myth that are related to the Christian story: descending to the underworld, dying, after three days being raised from the dead, and freeing the dead from the underworld.[10] This ancient story of the rescue of the dead continues in the Christian affirmation of Jesus' descent into hell. And the "food of life" and "the water of life" remind us of bread and water, which play significant parts in Christian worship. We even say that Jesus brings us new life and raises us from the dead.

To transvaluate this Christian proclamation and find the meaning for today requires that we accept the fact that the concept of a place under the earth called hell belongs to another age. We are not bound to the thought-forms and worldview of that day. We can no longer point up and down to designate heaven and hell without in some sense being schizoid, expressing our religious convictions with pre-scientific terms and living our secular lives with modern idioms. Yet, we can be sympathetic to the concern of the early Christians that those in the past are included in the grace disclosed in Jesus. But we do not need the descent into hell in any literal sense to affirm this. We can say that the love of God disclosed in Jesus is the way God has always been and now has been made clearer in Jesus' life. Those in the past are included because we have found in Jesus a love that is the same yesterday, today, and forever. What the early Christians were trying to do with mythology, we can affirm theologically. The reconciling and empowering love of God was focused in the human Jesus. He revealed the timelessness of God.

One thing more can be said about the descent into hell. Later theologizing was aware of all that Jesus experienced in his crucifixion experience. He was forsaken by most of his followers; he was obviously defeated in his mission to proclaim the kingdom of God; he saw no visible evidence that his mission would be continued; he was suffering through torture and rejection. This is indeed the experience of hell as separation. Jesus even experienced the agony of "My God, my God, why have you forsaken me?" Hell is a reality about life experienced by Jesus.

Outside Jerusalem was the Valley of Hinnom, called in Greek "Gehenna," where children in an earlier day were sacrificed. Gehenna was a refuse dump where the fires burned constantly to prevent pestilence. What an appropriate term for hell: the place of fire, stench, wretchedness, waste, loneliness, and separation from all that is best about human life. The vagueness of the name Sheol was replaced by Christians with Gehenna. Jesus descended into Gehenna. Jesus suffered the extremities of life to which we are subject, and he emerged victorious. What an affirmation! When we experience our hells, we know someone who was there before us, enabling us to realize some hope even in the worst circumstances.

Hell is separation from God, from others, and from self. All humans experience this state. Jesus did, and that makes a difference. The descent into hell can mean that Jesus experienced death as all humans do. The descent can also serve as a symbol that the past is not forsaken. Jesus' time in history is an event that reveals who God is. The descent is also the word that whatever extremity we go through has been experienced by the Man of Nazareth. This is what many believe about what they do not have to believe.[11]

– 10 –

The Resurrection
and Ascension

*A Christian does not have to believe that Jesus' physical
body was resurrected from the dead and later levitated, moving from earth up to heaven.*

*But Christians can believe that physical bodies are im-
portant; humans do not become disembodied spirits; Jesus'
physical body and ours have spiritual significance; and the
life of Jesus has been raised up over all lives as the exemplar.*

Each of the separate statements that begin these chapters has been the subject of controversy down through the
years. Christians do not agree theologically, and they never
have. The essence of Christianity is not in the literal truth of
the story language of the faith. In all of this I am pleading

that Christians not be divided over opinions about which obvious differences exist. Christians are united in the love of God revealed by Jesus, whom we call Christ, and not by our opinions.

We come now to two of the most controversial proclamations of Christians: that Jesus was resurrected from the dead and that he ascended into heaven. Yes, I believe. Yes, this is at the heart of the New Testament message. But, no, this does not mean that I, or many other Christians, believe in the resuscitation of a dead body or in a literal ascension. Physical bodies go the way of all organic material. Yes, I know the biblical passages that affirm physical appearances. These are apologetic words for the Docetists who did not accept that Jesus was physical at all. For them, he was a divine being in a kind of charade. But think of other passages: a "body" appearing in a room with the doors being closed, appearances where the "body" was not recognized, appearances only experienced by a select few and not by the many.

To read the Gospel accounts of the resurrection is to be made aware that there is no consistency in, no uniform understanding of, the resurrection experiences. The object here is to attempt to bring some clarity to the affirmation that Jesus was raised from the dead, but I am not living under any illusion that this will satisfy many readers. All of us must do our own theologizing while reflecting on this seminal Christian word.

Resurrection was not an uncommon word in that day. The idea that the dead body would rise again was common among primitive animists. Ancient burial customs often included tools and food for the dead. However we are not sure how literal this belief was or whether the ancients were able to differentiate between the physical and spiritual realities. Zoroastrianism was among the most materialistic of the ancient religions, but even this religion was not clear about whether the belief was in the raising of actual physical bodies. Jewish thought reacted against the Greek dualism of body and soul. In Greek thought, the higher rational power or soul had to be released from the body to attain its full life. Hebrew thought could not conceive of a soul having any meaning apart from a body. Thus the concept of resurrection involved the union of soul and body in order for there to be any life after death. One Jewish sect, the Pharisees, believed in the resurrection of the dead. The Sadducees did not. How literal this all was for Hebrew sages is not at all clear, and many scholars see this thought in more symbolic than literal terms.

Other religions have their resurrection stories. In the chapter on the virgin birth we referred to the Greek myth of Dionysus. Turning to this again, we discover a resurrection theme. Dionysus, the son of Zeus and the human princess Sebele, was killed by the Titans. Zeus raised him from the dead to become the divine god of the vine, symbolizing the cycle of vegetation. Egyptian mythology also has a resurrection. The Egyptian goddess Isis had a male consort, Osiris, who was a mortal ruler in ancient Egypt. When Osiris was torn to pieces, he was resurrected from the dead to become the god of the underworld.

What did the early Christians experience to which they gave the term *resurrection*? The earliest Christian writings were the letters of Paul. In Galatians he writes that God "was pleased to reveal his Son to me." His Damascus Road experience is recorded three times in Acts, but the accounts do not agree. In one account, those with him heard a voice but saw no one. In another they saw the light but did not hear a voice. The third account seems to focus on Paul's individual experience. (Acts 9:1–9; 22:3–11; 26:12–19) Paul refers to his conversion as a meeting with the risen Lord and equates his experience with that of Peter and the other disciples, justifying his own apostleship. (2 Cor. 15:5–8) Since Paul's experience was a spiritual and not a physical meeting with the risen Lord, we can assume that he regarded the other "appearances" as similar to his own.

What does all this mean about the resurrection? Some want to hold to the resurrection as a physical raising of a dead body. Others prefer to see this in the light of the thought-forms of that time which Christians used as vehicles to relate their experiences. The exact nature of those experiences may forever elude us, but I cannot help but make an attempt to understand the nature of two of them.

When Jesus met with the disciples in the Upper Room at what some think was a Seder meal, he did a most unusual thing. He varied the sacred Seder ritual (a totally unacceptable practice among the Jews) with this word at the traditional breaking of the bread: "Take, eat; this is my body." Then, with the traditional cup, another odd statement: "Drink of it, all of you; for this is my blood of the covenant." (Matt. 26:26–28) No wonder they were mystified. This was an intrusion into the Seder ritual, which was not to be tampered with. Following the meal, he was arrested, tried, tortured, crucified, dead, and buried. What did the disciples do? One account has them meeting on the evening of the first day of the week. Where? Perhaps back in the Upper Room to eat a meal together, which happens to most families after a funeral service. Who was the host at this meal? Perhaps it was Peter. Reading between the lines, I can picture a scenario. Peter picks up the bread to give the traditional Jewish blessing, and he suddenly remembers and repeats what he recalled: "This is my body." As they eat together, the doors being closed, Jesus appears in their midst. What was the experience? An apparition? I do not think so. A materialization of a spiritual body? I do not believe this, either. By the inspiration of God, the intrusion of the Spirit, they suddenly realized that it was not all over. The Lord was with them. They "saw" him in one another. The Lord had a new body, and they were the body. The only residuum of the resurrection (as my New Testament professor, John Knox, used to say) is the existence of the Church as the Body of Christ. Jesus is dead. Jesus has a new body.

They tried to kill the Christ, the activity of God; they could not. The Christ is raised in a new body.

Is this fanciful? Too rational an explanation of a mystery? Perhaps, but this makes more sense to me than the resuscitation of a body, which finally has to be explained away somehow. A similar explanation can be given to the Emmaus Road couple who recognized the Presence when they were seated together at a meal table. The Presence, then and now, gives to those who recognize the Risen Lord an identity, an empowerment, and a new community in the Spirit.

What do we say about all the other resurrection texts? I am convinced that Christians used the story form to assert their conviction emerging out of their real experience with a leader with whom they were still in relationship. We cannot know what actually happened, but we do know that the experiences were convincing to them.

What about the ascension? Some Christians believe literally that Jesus' resurrected body levitated and moved up into the sky to heaven. That as twenty-first-century people they can so believe is a mystery to me. Again we have an example of Christian midrash: the tying of a present experience to a past story. Elijah, that early prophet about whom many miracle stories are told, was taken by a whirlwind up into heaven. (2 Kings 2:11) In both stories, the experience was of not seeing a beloved leader anymore.

The ascension story (Acts 1:9), like the resurrection stories, is told in a very physical way. The reason for this has been mentioned. That Jesus was fully human and physical (and not a spiritual being playing like a human) was an important part of the Christian witness. Also, the cosmology of that day played a role in the way they wrote. They thought heaven was a place, close to earth, just above the "firmament," their name for the blue we see in the sky. (See the diagram on page 74.) God was "there," able to survey the whole scene on earth. A generation later, Christians af-

Old Cosmology

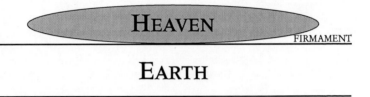

firmed their conviction that Jesus is Lord of Lords and King of Kings, that he is "high over all," and expressed this in the ascension story. What was behind their language we can still affirm today without accepting their cosmology. To make this story literal, or to claim, as one fundamentalist affirmed, "Jesus was the first astronaut," is, to my mind, intellectual and spiritual nonsense.

Heaven is not a geographical place. What happened to Jesus' body is an unanswerable question. But the experience of a living Lord and the conviction that death did not stop the activity of God in Jesus, are as true now as then. The ascension is not a movement into space but a testimony of Jesus' move into authority—sitting at the right hand of God (not, of course, literally but symbolically).

Both the resurrection and ascension stories affirm a great truth about life. Physical bodies are important; humans do not become disembodied spirits; Jesus' physical life and ours have spiritual significance; and the influence of our lives in the flesh does outlast us. The Body of Christ is still present in those people who in their physical lives attempt to follow the self-giving and compassionate life of Jesus. "He lives!" continues to be the great Christian affirmation. This is what many believe about what they do not have to believe.[11]

– 11 –

The Coming Again

A Christian does not have to believe that the physical, flesh-and-blood Jesus is coming back to earth again.

But Christians can believe that further "comings" are not unrelated to the first, and that whatever comes will be in harmony with that humanity represented in the fleshly life of Jesus.

In all but the first chapter, we have been examining what a Christian does not have to believe about the past. Now for two chapters we shall look at what a Christian does not have to believe about the future. Christians face the future affirming that Christ will come again. This is more often referred to as the second coming, a term not in the Christian Scriptures but first used by Justin Martyr in the second century. What do Christians believe about this second coming?

Some make this very literal, believing that the flesh-and-blood Jesus (or a glorified body) will return to earth and lead a victorious army to victory over the forces of evil. They have accepted the image of a military Messiah and affirm what Jesus himself chose not to be. This has led to all kinds of predictions about when this "event" would happen. I remember an upstate New York religious group whose members in 1936 sold homes and other possessions and gathered on a hill waiting for the Lord to return. They, of course, were mistaken and later formed a farming community in the area. Similar happenings have often occurred elsewhere.

Perhaps the most popular of those who take the second coming literally has been Hal Lindsey. In his book *The Late Great Planet Earth*,[13] first published in 1970, with over a million copies sold in three years, he predicted that the second coming would occur in 1988. With an eisegesis (reading into the Scripture preconceived notions) and not exegesis (finding in the Scripture what is there) and also a false understanding of biblical prophecy (fore-telling, not forthtelling), he butresses his arguments to assert with certainty the date of Christ's return. He affirms a closed universe perspective, everything being pre-determined. Humans are mere puppets or pawns in the hands of the Almighty. He asserts in his book that nationalism is the best posture. It is fruitless to work for a better world. The United Nations is useless and unnecessary. All efforts to improve the lot of humans in this world are wasted. The Lord is going to return in 1988 to put an end to present orders.

This is the most socially unproductive and irresponsible position to take in the relationship between Church and society. And to think that in the seventies and eighties we had political figures who espoused this point of view. Such obsession with the literal and physical second coming has, through the ages, siphoned off creative energy into useless prognostication with date projections. How socially and spiritually unproductive this has been!

An open universe is one in which human choices make a difference. All is not pre-determined, as the poet Omar Khayyam expressed in this quatrain:

> 'Tis all a Chequer-board of Nights and Days
> Where Destiny with Men for Pieces plays:
> Hither and thither moves, and mates, and slays,
> And one by one back in the Closet lays.

No, we have roles to play in the human enterprise. This means that our decisions make a difference. In this understanding, humans are dignified as being co-workers with God in perfecting a creation that is still on the way toward completion. As Christians we do not have to believe that a literal second coming is on the way so that all we need to do is wait for the inevitable. The Hebrews, under the spell of the Exodus, awaited a further deliverance which they called "The Day of the Lord." This was modified later by apocalyptic thought (espousing a soon-to-be climactic end to history) to the idea of a personal Messiah. The coming of the Messiah was a controversial subject, with some expecting a revival of the Davidic dynasty, others looking for the arrival of the Son of Man as a spiritual being, and still others holding that no Messiah would be coming. Political, ethical, and apocalyptic ideas mingle in a confusing fashion in the Hebrew Scriptures.

The early Christians had an eschatological perspective. The parousia (presence or coming) was part of that early witness. But what that coming would be is quite ambiguous. This is especially true about John's Gospel, which seems to identify the coming at one time with the resurrection, at another with the gift of the Spirit, and at another with the death of the believer. Paul appears in his letters to believe in a dramatic return; but when some took him literally, he seemed to shy away from any immediacy. In Ephesians and the later letters, eschatology (concern with end things) was eclipsed by ecclesiology (practical church matters). In 2 Peter, we find a skepticism arising from the mistaken hope of a literal return. Obviously life was going on, and the early hopes of an immediate return faded. Some are reluctant to see that the early hope was symbolic and not literal. Others are convinced that whatever literalism appears in the writings was the temporal garb of Christians caught up in the dramatic excitement of the new life they were experiencing.

Many today hold a disdain for eschatology and all matters dealing with the end of history as we know it. The power of science and all our technological progress has brought so many new possibilities to the fore. Genetic engineering, organ transplants, computer programming, bio-engineering, life extension, and much more have enriched the lives of many. At the same time, unfortunately, the glorification of consumption, raucous entertainment, flamboyant media displays of violence, and waning of ethical standards have helped to stimulate a materialistic and hedonistic culture. So many want to eat, drink, and be merry, focusing on gratification now. Yet, this has tended to obscure the fact that wholeness of life, healing of mind and spirit as well as body, and the unity of humanity on planet earth are missing from our experiences.

What, then, does this coming again mean for those who do not take it literally but try to take it seriously? Is there another perspective on the second coming that could help us come to fullness of life? I believe so. The readiness and anticipatory stance are important parts of Christian living. We live between the past and the future, and we draw from both. The past informs us that God has been working to create a people who are blessed in order to be a blessing. People have been brought together from isolated families to tribes, from tribes to communities, from communities to states, from states to nations, and from nations to groups of nations. When will we be one humanity of mutually dependent people on planet earth? The past helps us to see a future evolving toward a more humanized life on this planet. God continues to break into life in reconciling and redemptive ways. God's presence is often hidden in the present; but when we look back, many of us are able to say God was there, but we or they did not see God at the time. The past helps us to look forward to the future in hope.

Do I believe in the second coming? Yes, and in successive comings that stand for the anticipatory element in the Christian faith. Do I believe in the return of the physical or glorified Jesus? No, I do not. When I say, "Come, Lord Jesus!" I am saying with Christians down through the ages, "Come into my life; come into our lives; come, O Christ!" This is a prayer for the activity of God represented and demonstrated in Jesus. The meaning of the coming again is that God is the Presence ever coming to push us to complete the work begun, that what is coming is the Christ (the loving and reconciling activity of God). The final coming is at the center of the Christian faith and is the symbol of the boundary of human experience in time, space, and eternity.

This is what many believe about what they do not have to believe.[12]

– 12 –

Life after Death

A Christian does not have to believe that life after death means a continued existence with consciousness of self and others.

But Christians can believe that our state after death is in the hands of a loving God, that we have no need for fear or apprehension, that in the all-encompassing love of God we shall never not have been.

Are you saved? Are you going to heaven? At one time these seemed to be one and the same question. The image of heaven was a place of eternal happiness and peace where all the injustices of life would be overcome and where at death we would be reconciled with our loved ones who preceded us. More and more people are seeing heaven as a state of being that is related to the here and now, whatever it may mean about life after death. John Wesley, in writing about

Ephesians 2:8, said this: "The salvation which is here spoken of is not what is frequently understood by that word, the going to heaven, eternal happiness. . . . It is not a blessing which lies on the other side of death; or (as we usually speak) in the other world. . . . It is not something at a distance: it is a present thing; a blessing which, through the free mercy of God, ye are now in possession of." [14] Heaven for Wesley was more related to this life than the next, though he believed in life after death. For Wesley the essence of heaven was to "see God, to know God, to love God."

One of the troublesome problems of religious people today is living in the twenty-first century while using the cosmological language of the first century. See the diagram on age 74 to get a picture of that early cosmology. Note that heaven was conceived as a sphere above the firmament (the blue up there) and was the dwelling place of God. The firmament separated the water above the earth from that on or below the earth. Hell (sheol), at the other extreme, was a subterranean cavern under the earth where the shades of humans went after they died. To go to sheol was simply to die, in pre-exile Hebrew thinking. The concepts of heaven and hell as places of rewards and punishments came to us from Persia and the religion of Zoroaster. According to Zoroaster, the soul after death remains three days with the body to meditate on deeds. On the fourth day, the soul journeys to the place of judgment. Mithra, the ancient god of the Aryans, judges. The good are sent to paradise or heaven with maidens escorting those so blessed. Paradise is described as a place of beauty, light, pleasant scents, and noble spirits.

The evil ones are sent to hell to be confined forever with stench and unimaginable horrors. The Hebrews brought such mythological concepts with them from Babylonia, which are reflected in post-exile writings.

People still think of heaven being up and hell down. If pressed, most people recognize both up and down as symbols or metaphors. We know today that a line pointing down goes right through the earth and is as up as our traditional designation for heaven. We need a new way of speaking in order to speak clearly to the people of our time. See the diagram on page 84 for one attempt to find a new symbol that is more in harmony with present-day cosmology. Note the historical line from birth to death. See also that heaven is a perpendicular reality intersecting life at every point. In the words of a Christian tradition called "creation spirituality," this is God in everything and everything in God. With pleasant experiences or ecstasies we can imagine how we accept life and, here and there, experience heaven. The birth of a child, a moment of reconciliation, a fulfilling sex experience, a scene of natural beauty, a time of creativity, a job well done, a new insight from an author or speaker, and much more can be heavenly experiences. But how about the tragedies, the sorrows, the defeats, the unfulfilled moments, the misunderstandings, and the separations? These can be experiences of hell that take us away from life in negative spirals of self-depreciation, rejection of life, alcohol or drug addiction, depression, and the like. These are the arrows pointing away from life. Heaven is the experience of being reconciled to life in whatever the experience, while hell is separation from life.

I have never seen this so well presented as in the film *Zorba the Greek,* based on the novel by Nikos Kazantzakis. As I remember the film (and this will be with some liberties), an Englishman and Zorba enter a business venture on a Greek island. Zorba's task is to find a way to get lumber from a mountain down to the valley without modern equipment. He proceeds to build, with the help of townspeople, an extensive cable railway system from the mountain to the valley. While the project is in process, the Englishman develops a relationship with a young woman who is killed by a mob. The Englishman is beside himself with grief and cannot seem to engage again with life. Zorba tries every way to entice him back into life. Finally he says something like this:

Old Cosmology

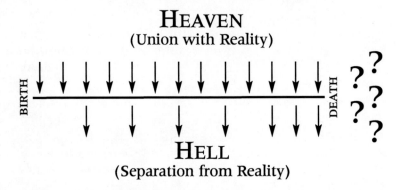

HEAVEN
(Union with Reality)

HELL
(Separation from Reality)

"Boss, years ago I had a son who died young. Do you know what I did?"

"No, what?" the Englishman responded.

"I danced!" was the response.

"You did what?"

"I danced! What should I have done? Moped and felt sorry for myself? No! Life was still good, and I could live with the inevitable."

Later the cable system was complete, and everyone gathered to see the logs come down from the mountain to the valley. After an initial log or two, the conveyance began to shake and suddenly the whole contraption collapsed with a roar. Zorba and his boss viewed the scene, both aware that the success of the venture depended on the success of this conveyance. They looked at each other knowing that their business venture, and likely their relationship, was over. Zorba simply exclaimed, "Wasn't that a splendiferous crash!" The boss looked intently at Zorba and, understanding for the first time that life can be lived fully in the midst of any circumstance, he blurted out, "Zorba, teach me to dance." The film ends with the two dancing on the beach to the Greek music.

Heaven is present in the midst of life to those who are willing to accept reality and live with it. Resources are available to help us respond in faith and confidence to whatever happens. Hell is the rejection of life, running away from what has been given. John Wesley expressed it this way: ". . . if there were no other hell, thou hast hell enough within thee. An awakened conscience is hell. Pride, envy, wrath, hatred, malice, revenge—what are these but hell upon earth."[15] *Heaven* and *hell* can be meaningful terms to address faithful and unfaithful responses to life. Is there more than heaven and hell in this life? What about life after death?

John Wesley was convinced that what we experience in this life is but a foretaste of what is to come. The question for him was not whether heaven and hell await us in the afterlife but whether we experience heaven or hell now. Wesley does not deal with the tragedies like the famine-ridden hordes in Africa or the sufferings of destitute refugees, the victims of political and ethnic strife. Such injustices remain for me among the most troublesome situations for Christian theologizing and Christian action.

Heaven or life after death can well be a part of Christian hope for those who find this congenial; but heaven cannot be the object of faith. Faith has one object—God. If we have had some experience of the love of God, we can trust that whatever God has in store for us is good. When someone quotes to me John 14:2 ("In my Father's house are many rooms . . .") and asks what this means, I simply say that I do not believe that this was meant to be a geography of heaven. This means to me that there as an at-home-ness to death. There is no need to fear the ending of life. Christians will relate differently to this subject. Some will hold out for a life after death in which we will recognize and be recognized, though what this means in terms of disembodied spirits was a mystery to Wesley and is now to me.

I turn to the words of a Jewish pianist, Artur Rubinstein, for an insightful word. On his ninetieth birthday, he was interviewed by CBS. One of the questions asked was, "Do you believe in life after death?" He responded, "No, I don't think so. If I did and it were not so, I would be very disappointed. But if it is so, I shall be delighted."

I do not know for sure about life after death. I do know something of heaven and hell in this life. I have experienced them both. I live by faith in the love of God. What is ahead for us we can leave in God's hands. Some may want more than this and may hope for more; but, for numerous Christians, making life after death an absolute is more than is warranted. This is what many believe about what they do not have to believe.

– 13 –

The Trinity

A Christian does not have to believe that the Trinity is an accurate portrayal of the nature of God.

But Christians can believe that the Trinity has to do with the nature of how God has been experienced, instead of an attempt to describe the essence of God.

The idea of God and the nature of God are subjects that far exceed the purpose of this book. Yet we cannot discuss the Trinity without some consideration of God questions. What immediately follows is preparation for considering the doctrine of the Trinity and the role that this concept can play in the life of Christians.

Does God exist?

This is a meaningless question to me. Does being exist? I am. One day I shall not be. The term *God* does not refer to a being alongside other beings. God is the ground of being, the origin of being, the sustainer of being, the One who holds it all together. Without God nothing would be. I am aware of sharing in a historical process that includes being. What is behind the process and its ongoingness is God. Neither the process itself nor the universe is eternal. This would be pantheism. God is the transcendent reality behind it all.

Concepts of God have changed through the years, and they need to change. We are growing in our perception of the nature of God. No longer do most of us live with a concept of God as a being up there like a puppeteer, every now and then pulling a string to make something happen down here, or not pulling a string and leaving us wondering what God is doing. Nor do most of us attribute to God all the natural disasters or the inhumanities that seem to plague the human community. Elie Wiesel, Nobel peace prize winner, author, teacher, lecturer, and a holocaust survivor, tells the story of a trial of God held by a group of Jews in a concentration camp. A rabbi served as the presiding judge, and prosecuting and defense attorneys presented their cases. The end result was conviction. God was sentenced to death. After the verdict, the rabbi judge announced that it was time for evening prayer. What this story tells us is that ideas of God can die, but the search for faith and ultimate meaning continue. Also, the story makes clear that we can be angry about the way life is, angry with God as we understand God, but because God is God, God can endure our anger.

Can I prove God?

None of the above is proof to the rational mind. If I

could take whatever makes up God and, in scientific fashion, prove God, I would instead be proving that I am superior to God, that I am master of that which constitutes God. I can take water and by electrolysis prove that water is composed of two parts hydrogen and one part oxygen. I have, at the same time, proved that water is subject to me, for I am able to take it apart and put it back together. God is not amenable to me and to my scientific methods.

If God, why evil?

Creation is not complete; it is becoming. "In the beginning when God began to create the heavens and the earth" is also a proper translation of Genesis 1. What would life be like if all were perfect goodness, perfectly related, perfectly functioning? Some might consider this a "consummation devoutly to be wished." Such a life, for me and others, would remove the element of challenge. In creating creatures who share in God's nature (a faith statement), God became self-limited in order to give us freedom to be, to do, and to become. The process of becoming is the great drama of life. We make mistakes, we suffer, creation suffers. Are we learning? Are we moving on to something greater that we can yet be? I believe the possibility is here, but there is no guarantee. The agony of our imperfection is part of our not having arrived.

Human evil is the result of free will. Humans can go "wrong" or "right." I cannot imagine a creature that is free but has no possibility of evil. If one is free to be good, that one is also free to be bad. Free will is what makes evil possible but is also that which makes love, goodness, and joy worth having. These are the products of free will overcoming separateness and suspicion, selfishness and greed, and disharmony and disunity. Do we have the freedom to destroy not only ourselves but the earth? This must be so. Paul

Tillich once observed in a seminary class (when confronted with a question about the possibility of the destruction of all life on earth) that no matter the tragedy, life has been worth it. Once in the whole process of geologic time, a creature did exist that at his/her best moments expressed the loving and creative process at the heart of life.

Do we need God?

Suppose no intelligence is beyond the universe, no creative mind. If so, no one designed my brain for thinking. Evolution proceeded, and when the atoms in my skull, for chemical or other physical reasons, arranged themselves in a certain way, I was given the by-product of thought. If so, how can I trust my own thinking, which has emerged by chance or accident, to be true? If I cannot trust my own thinking to be true, I cannot depend on arguments leading to atheism, or on anything else to be true. Unless I trust in God (in purpose, plan, and design), I cannot trust in reason. Our rational powers make no sense to me apart from Universal Thought, in which my thought participates. I cannot believe in human life and thought being just an accidental collocation of atoms. And I am glad to find numerous scientists today (such as Freeman Dyson in his book *Infinite in All Directions*) who feel the same way.[16]

Is God personal, aware of me?

I am aware of the mysterious process of life, of sharing in being. Am I greater than the process of which I am a part? That makes no sense to me, for that would make the part greater than the whole. Whatever consciousness or awareness means, it has emerged from a universal consciousness (or ground of consciousness), the mystery of which is be-

yond my comprehension. As far back as we have any historical records and in the mythology of all ancient peoples, we
discover the leap from personal consciousness to an awareness of something beyond. This does not prove anything but
points us toward a transcendent reality.

Who is God?

Finally, in this preparation for considering the concept of
Trinity, I affirm that God is Presence—a loving, caring, compassionate Presence. This involves a leap of faith, which is
not subject to proof. Some cannot make this leap. They cannot disprove God any more than I can prove God. I respect
them for their honesty in spite of cultural pressures. Yet, I
feel that something is missing for them. Faith gives us the
confident assurance of a Presence. Is there an objective reality behind this subjective assurance? I cannot be absolutely
sure. But I find it difficult to believe that a basic human
hunger (a reaching out for that which began and continues
to sustain life) is unrelated to reality.

A famous English atheist, whose wife died, wrote in his
diary: "I thank ———— that I ever knew her." He was char-
acteristically honest, but he was reaching out—a natural
hunger for the source of all being. That hunger is assuaged,
for me, in God.

What does all this have to do with the Trinity? The
Christian doctrine of the Trinity is an attempt to explain the
unexplainable. Who can really make sense out of this—God
in three persons? John Wesley wrote two centuries ago: "I
dare not insist upon anyone's using the word 'Trinity' or
'Person.' I use them myself without any scruple . . . but if
any man has any scruple concerning them, who can con-
strain him to use them? I cannot." [17] Although he affirmed
that the three bear witness, Father, Son, and Holy Ghost,

and that the three are one, he did not count it important to believe any explication of the terms.

The doctrine is not explicitly stated anywhere in Scripture, although there are suggestive passages. The doctrine goes back to Tertullian at the beginning of the third century and found expression at the Council of Nicaea in 325 C.E. The East and West argued for years on the meaning. The doctrine really says more about human experience than it does about God. Christians did and do experience the creator God (Father and Mother), God revealed in the life and ministry of Jesus, and a continuing Presence. Again, experience precedes doctrine. The question is: How do you experience God?

The Trinity has been the most universally accepted description of the human experience of God. A decade or two ago, some theologians were expressing regrets about the practical irrelevance of trinitarian language. But in recent years the Trinity is getting renewed attention. A recent "Trinity Summit" was held, focused on recovering the doctrine. But is the trinitarian language today acceptable and helpful? Some would say yes, while others would disagree. "Saint Augustine said that Christians used the concept and the word 'Trinity' because it was a little better than saying nothing, when one had to say something." [18]

The Hindus have a Trimurti (Trinity) of Brahma, Shiva, and Vishnu, who are not seen as separate. The substance is one but the gods are three. Both Trinity and Trimurti point to the complex nature of God. In Christian theology the threefold terms for God are not a numerical plurality but a matter of facets, or distinct but not separate aspects, of the Divine. To try to define any expression of the Divine leads one to multi-faceted language. The closer we get to God, the more we begin to see that what appeared to be One is many-sided. Can this be essentially what the Trinity is all about?

Should Christians agree today on their beliefs about the Trinity? The fact is that they do not. Some view the Trinity as a vestigial remnant of past debates. Others are rigid trinitarians, believing that the Trinity is of the essence of God. Yet, for many Christians, trinitarian doctrine is simply the grammar of divine identity—the framework by which to understand the Christian faith. God has more than one way of being God; and Father, Son, and Holy Spirit are the terms for saying so. From this perspective, the Trinity is the interpretation of what happened and continues to happen in and through the event known as Jesus Christ. In spite of Jesus crucified, dead, and buried, a Spirit has been let loose in the world. That Spirit is still present and is none other than the continuing expression of God's self-actualization. But the Trinity is not a necessary belief but an option that many Christians find helpful in describing experiences of God.

At least this is what many believe about what they do not have to believe.

– 14 –

Satan

A Christian does not have to believe that Satan (the Devil) is an actual personal being causing the evil in the world.

But Christians can believe that Satan is a symbol of the opposition to God's purposes for human life.

The word *satan* means "adversary." *Satan* is first used in the Hebrew Scriptures relative to ordinary human adversaries. The Philistines feared that David would be their satan. When Solomon was in power, the word was that no satan was left to oppose him. In early Hebrew writings, satan was not a personified spiritual being but a common word for the adversary, whoever that might have been. The personification of Satan came into Hebrew from the Zoroastrian *Shaitin*, which was another term for Angra Mainyu, or Ahriman, the evil spirit. In the Hebrew Bible's post-exilic writing, Satan became the adversary of humanity and the accuser of humanity before God.

Devil is the English translation of the Greek *diabolos*, meaning "slanderer," one against us. As the chief of evil demons, the Devil, in later Jewish and early Christian usage, was identified with Satan. As the source of all evil, the Devil was intent on the enslavement of humanity. The Devil is presented in the Christian Scriptures as the tempter of Jesus, the head of opposition to his ministry, the "prince of the power of the air" (Ephesians 2:2), and the author of the bloody persecution feared by the author of Revelation. The Devil has figured conspicuously in Christian speculation, though his power is always presented as being undermined by Christ. Satan and the Devil are the two terms used by which evil has been personified as the adversary of God. Each in its own way points to that which is in opposition to God's purposes.

Many Christians speak quite literally about Satan or the Devil, using the terms interchangeably. In fundamentalist writings, demons and Satan as the prince of demons are actual created beings who have fallen from their original angelic states. Satan was, in this view, the greatest of the angels and desired to be like God. His pride brought about his rebellion, and he was cast forth from heaven, according to the apocalyptic book of Ezekiel. Satan, according to the biblical literalists, is a being whose agenda is to deceive humanity and to work in opposition to God's purposes.

People are, of course, free to believe whatever is congenial to their mental processes; but this literal understanding of Satan misses the whole nature of mythology. Mythological writing is neither factual nor historical but symbolic. The effort in mythology is to express in highly symbolic ways an understanding of some of the most profound issues of human life. Why evil? Why are we tempted to deny our creatureliness and to play God over our lives and the lives of others? Why that common human experience expressed by the Apostle Paul: ". . . for I do not do the good I want, but the evil I do not want is what I do"? (Romans 7:19) What is the activity of grace that brings reconciliation and redemption? Such questions elude factual or even psychological answers. Mythology leads us into deeper levels of perception. No one has to take the Satan or the Devil literally. Just as no one has to take the salvation metaphors (diagram page 4) literally.

I accept mythological explanations for what they are: human efforts to deal with life's mysteries. At the same time, being a rational creature, I have had to ponder on these things. I prefer to think of the original nothingness or chaos, out of which God brought something into being, as the prevailing temptation. Without God's sustaining power, all would once again be chaos. Chaos is the continual threat to humanity and is a strangely powerful attraction. Who has not been tempted to destroy self? Or what is child or spouse abuse but a reversion to a more primitive life, closer to the original chaos? In the midst of life we face opposition that endangers the purpose of God, which, it seems to me, is to produce a people who embody God's nature, which is caring love.

Satan, or the Devil, is a symbol of that opposition to God. Satan is that which hides God from us, stands between us and God's purpose for us. I like to think not of a being, nor of the fallen angel of mythology (which has its non-literal truth), but of the emptiness or nothingness that is separate from God's creative, self-giving, and reconciling love. Whatever hides that from us is our adversary and God's. That is Satan. I am convinced that Mahatma Gandhi was partially right when he wrote someplace: "The only devils in the world are those running around in our own hearts, and that is where our battles should be fought."[19] This does does not deal with the subject of systemic evil, about which Paul is concerned with his "principalities and powers," but Gandhi's words are a good beginning as we come to terms with our own foibles.

Some Christians may choose to be more literal in their beliefs. Why? I do not know. There is nothing absolute about the Devil (Satan), either the term or the experienced reality to which the symbol points. This is what many Christians believe about what they do not have to believe.

– 15 –

Essential Christian Convictions

Having spent fourteen chapters on what Christians do not have to believe, coupled with what many Christians believe about what they do not believe, two questions should be raised: What do you believe is basic Christianity? What are the essentials of Christian belief? Many will find these statements and their fuller explication inadequate. I simply assert that these are adequate for me to be a Christian. They are what I perceive to be essential, but I make no claim to them being absolute, complete, or all-encompassing. I find the following affirmations in harmony with the basic beliefs of my own denomination, even though in many cases the beliefs are expressed differently. In dialogue with others, I have discovered that what I am saying here can be expressed in numerous ways. I respect the views of others, even though I may not always find them congenial to my thinking processes. I ask for, but will not always get, the same respect for my opinions.

Here are my essential Christian beliefs.

God is the object of faith, a transcendent dimension of life not amenable to our physical senses; and Jesus (called Christ) is the lens through which I see God.

This is related to my early definition of a Christian as one for whom Jesus Christ plays the definitive role in life. That role points us toward God, the object of faith; and in that role Jesus both tells and shows us what to do in relation to that Object. This means that it is not what we believe intellectually but what we trust in and rely upon. For me God can be trusted to be God: the Mystery of love that can be experienced. All the salvation or atonement metaphors mentioned in the Introduction point to this definitive role. Whatever they may mean to others, they are for me testimonies of faith emerging from the experiences of early Christians. In the revelation of God found in the life and death of Jesus, and in that experience they called the resurrection, those early Christians found themselves given new life, hope, and empowerment. He saved them from a lesser life and gave them a fuller life.

What was the lesser life from which he saved them? In the terms I have already used in previous pages, he saved those early Christians from absolutizing a relative good and saved them for a life filled by the awareness of unbounded love. And what did those early Christians tend to absolutize? Some literalized and made absolute the Law and the Prophets, which was the Bible in Jesus' time. Jesus relativized the Scriptures: "They said of old . . . but I say to you . . ." Others absolutized their own health and were not able to live with their infirmities. Jesus set many free. "Rise, take up your pallet, and walk." (John 5:8) Others absolutized their rational powers and wanted to accept nothing but what was in harmony with their own philosophical presuppositions, like the Epicurean and Stoic philosophers of Athens. (Acts 17:16 ff.) Others absolutized their racial and ethnic origins and lived prejudiced against those different from them. Jesus broke their stereotypes and responded to all people as persons dignified by being human. Some absolutized sex roles and attempted to maintain male supremacy and to keep women submissive. Jesus was the first feminist, as seen in his relationships with Mary and Martha, Mary Magdalene, and the woman at the well. Jesus was more concerned about hypocrisy, self-righteousness, and materialism than he was about sexual matters. Can anyone really imagine Jesus being as unloving and prejudicial toward homosexuals, as many are in our society?

What has all this to do with you and me? We are also absolutizers. We do it with the Bible, our moral standards, our work, our play, our children, our mates, our finances, our health, and many, many other aspects of our lives. Jesus is Savior by placing us in touch with the one absolute, God, and God is love. With love at the center we are set free from making absolute anything less. Jesus Christ is God's agent of salvation (healing and wholeness). This does not necessarily mean the only agent. Yet, Jesus has functioned as an agent of salvation in an amazing way down through the centuries. All this is consistent with what is the earliest Christian creed: Jesus Christ is Lord, or Jesus Christ our Lord.

A source of love exists in this world that transcends all the changing circumstances of our lives.

I believe it; I experience it. This, of course, follows the first belief logically. What I see in Jesus is an awareness of this love. The way he lived and the way he died authenticate the presence of a love from which we cannot be separated by anything that happens to us. With Paul I have been enabled to say "that neither death, nor life, nor angels, nor principalities, nor things present, nor things to come, nor powers, nor height, nor depth, nor anything else in all creation, will be able to separate us from the love of God in Christ Jesus our Lord." (Romans 8:38–39) This conviction has come to me within the community of the Christian faith, which has exposed me to the story of Jesus of Nazareth. Others may not be so moved; I have been.

Faith (trust) in this source of love is justified in human experience.

Although faith is not the product of reason, it is not irrational. The lack of faith, however, has consequences. Basically it means that any trust one has in life, in others, in the processes of the natural world is unsubstantiated and leads quite naturally to insecurity. Wherever there is a trusting commitment to ultimate reason, support, and the meaning of life, we can assert the essence of a belief in God or a trust in something transcendent. (I am dependent here on what has become a definitive book on Christianity to emerge in my generation, namely, *On Being a Christian* by Hans Kung.) There are believers in God who do not know that they are. I have discovered in some atheists a level of trust that is missing in some Christians. This leads me to say that there are some who are "in" who are really "out" and some who are "out" (in any formal religious sense) who are really "in."

A person who affirms God, the reality that is the object of Jesus' faith, knows why he/she trusts reality. Those who cannot trust reality, or the way life is, are very likely "exposed quite personally to the danger of ultimate abandonment, menace and decay, resulting in doubt, fear, even despair. All this is true, of course, only if the atheism is quite serious and not an intellectual pose, snobbish caprice or thoughtless superficiality."[18] (This is not to say that all true atheists are in despair.) On the other hand, "Belief in God is nourished by an ultimately substantiated basic trust: when [one] assents to God, [one] opts for an ultimate reason, support, meaning of reality."[20] Does this prove itself in the living? I assert from experience that it does. For me such basic trust is justified.

Creation is good; the physical is a channel of the spirit; human life has eternal meaning; and each individual has a role to play in the ongoing human enterprise.

Such a conviction dignifies human life. Again, nothing is proved by such a conviction; but those who earnestly can make such an affirmation are saved from negativity: being chronic malcontents, moving into a downward spiral of self-depreciation, becoming fatalists or cynics, and adopting the view of life expressed by Shakespeare's Macbeth, namely, that life is " a tale told by an idiot, full of sound and fury, signifying nothing." (V.v.)

The above Christian conviction is, of course, shared by others, but it has come to me through a Christianity that flows out of the understanding of life exemplified in Jesus of Nazareth.

In spite of fading human memories and the physical inconsequence of any life, in the all-encompassing love of God, everyone is kept throughout eternity.

Again nothing is proved here, and I am not sure why this conviction is important to me. Perhaps it is human pride and the wish not to be forgotten. Perhaps it is rooted in the understanding of the uniqueness of each human being. Perhaps it is taking seriously the words of Jesus that God is aware of the sparrow's fall and how much more God must be aware of the creatures made in God's image.

However this conviction has come to me, it gives me an eternal perspective and further dignifies all human life.

Christianity is basically a social entity that unites individuals in a community of faith which has symbols and stories that define the course of life and illuminate the meanings in the capricious nature of human existence.

I am convinced that our relationship to God cannot be separated from our relationship to others. "[F]or those who do not love a brother or sister whom they have seen, cannot love God whom they have not seen." (1 John 4:20) Jesus put the love of God and neighbor as two parts of the same Commandment and thereby summarized the law. An individualized and privatized faith is only a part of Christianity. John Wesley told his people that "Christianity is essentially a social religion"[21] and that there is "no holiness but social holiness."[22] The acceptance of the Christian faith places us in a community that, led by Paul, calls itself the Body of Christ. Each one is a part of the body, and we need one another.

That community has a story, a magnificent and wondrous story, of God's involvement in human life. This story, told from Genesis to Revelation, unites historical events with a mythology that probes deeply into the basic human issues. This story has elements that touch us all when we do not get bogged down in a literalism that stultifies the message of faith. The symbols and stories developed by this community of faith still have power to lift human life from meaningless meandering into worship that confirms our identity, study that sensitizes us to the relationship between faith and life, and service that enables us to make a difference in the world.

Addendum

What about the traditional creeds? I affirm the creeds wholeheartedly, as many Christians do, without believing literally every affirmation. They contain profound truths that I have attempted to explicate in this book. The creeds are landmark documents from the past that express how people back then tried to communicate the faith in the language and thought-forms of that day. They are valuable statements and serve as teaching tools and also are helpful in encouraging dialogue. I wrote a book taking seriously the Apostles' Creed and its relevance for today[11]; but I refuse to absolutize creeds or see them as juridical norms for determining who is or is not a Christian. Does the life and death of Jesus, and the resurrection (however you understand that term), define your life? Then, we are Christians together. Let us not, for differences of opinion, destroy the unity that God has given us.

Appendix:
Group Study Sessions

Session 1

Present the role of believing in Christianity and the difference between faith and belief; what Christians believe about Jesus (essentials and non-essentials); salvation theories as metaphors emerging out of experience. (Preface and Introduction, pages. vii–16.)

Session 2

Explore the contemporary metaphors (Unsaved and Saved Lives) found with diagrams on pages 8–12. These attempt to transvaluate the old expressions of the faith. Are they true to that faith? Then discuss the difference between events and stories as found on pages 12–16.

Session 3

On the next page are fourteen statements about what a Christian does not have to believe, according to the writer. Go through these one by one to see if there is any consensus. (The statements can be duplicated.) Raise these possible questions about each statement:

1. What is the major issue behind the statement?
2. Is the belief historically relative to the cosmology, anthropology, or psychology of another day?
3. What is the personal value in believing in such a statement?
4. If the statement is not believed literally, is the Christian faith jeopardized in some way?
5. Is it possible that not believing the statement literally can lead to a more profound truth instead of mere credulity?

In reference to the latter question, what might that truth be?

Make a list of those statements which raised the most questions, were most troublesome, or those which the group wants to consider further. Assign chapters to be read to correspond to the group's interests. Pick and choose the chapters depending on the number of sessions you plan to have.

A Christian Does Not Have to Believe

1. That the Bible contains the literal words of God.
2. That Adam and Eve were historically the first two humans and that creation occurred in six days or even six thousand years.
3. That God at one time spoke audible words to Abraham, Moses, etc.
4. That at Moses' decree the Nile turned to blood and various plagues afflicted Egypt, contravening the laws of nature.
5. That angels were visible spiritual creatures who spoke audible words to Mary and Joseph.
6. That Jesus was conceived as a biological miracle without a human father.

7. That the miracles told about Jesus' life and death were historical happenings.

8. That the shedding of Jesus' blood has some miraculous power in itself.

9. That after he died Jesus went to hell to preach to the lost of the past.

10. That Jesus' physical body was resurrected from the dead and later levitated, moving from earth up to heaven.

11. That the physical, flesh-and-blood Jesus is coming back to earth again.

12. That life after death means a continued existence with consciousness of self and others.

13. That the Trinity is an accurate portrayal of the nature of God.

14. That the Devil (Satan) is an actual personal being causing the evil in the world.

Session 4

Following this page are fourteen statements about what a Christian can believe about the previous statements of what a Christian does not have to believe. At this session, use these to explore the possible depth meanings behind many traditional Christian beliefs. Raise these questions about each of the positive statements:

1. Does this statement get at the real meaning behind the belief? If not, what is the significance of the belief for today?

2. Is there some value in merely believing something to be true that is at variance with rational thinking?

3. Do the statements about what Christians can believe do some injustice to the Christian faith?

4. What relevance can the supernatural aspects of the belief statements have for twenty-first-century people?

5. Could these positive statements be true to the experience of those who gave us this record from the past?

What a Christian Can Believe

1. That the Bible becomes the Word of God, as time and again it enters into dialogue with us, leading us to significant insights and/or profound changes in our lives.

2. That Adam and Eve are symbolic figures, representing every man and woman, and the creation story affirms design and plan.

3. That biblical conversations with God represent that inner dialogue between the individuals and the divine will.

4. That the Moses stories point to a remarkable figure in history and assert his powerful influence.

5. That angels are the messengers in life who offer both presence and supportive help that radically change life situations.

6. That Jesus was unique and special, a one-of-a-kind representative of a higher dimension of life.

7. That the followers of Jesus experienced new life and used bodily health and nature symbols to express the radical changes they experienced.

8. That blood is a symbol of life, and Jesus' life has had a powerful influence upon the world.

9. That those in the past are included in God's seeking love, and His Christ activity is the same yesterday, today, and forever.

10. That physical bodies are important; humans do not become disembodied spirits; Jesus' physical body and ours have spiritual significance; and the life of Jesus is raised up as exemplar.

11. That further "comings" are not unrelated to the first, and that whatever comes will be in harmony with what was represented in Jesus.

12. That what is after death is in the hands of a loving God, and that in the all-encompassing love of God we shall ever be.

13. That the trinity has to do with the nature of how God

has been experienced instead of an attempt to describe the essence of God.

14. That the Devil (Satan) is a symbol of the opposition to God's purposes for human life.

Session 5

Plan the number of sessions to include the chapters in which your group has the most interest. In each case, compare the traditional statement with the transvaluated one. Is the modern one true to the faith? Go to the chapter material for the rationale. Leave time to discuss the essential Christian convictions found in Chapter 15. You may want to have a separate session on these. A good assignment would be to have each one in the group make up his/her own set of convictions.

Chapter Headings for Possible Class Use

1

The Bible as the Word of God

A Christian does not have to believe that the Bible contains the literal words of God.

But Christians can believe that the Bible becomes the word of God as time and again it enters into dialogue with us, leading us to significant insights and/or profound changes in our lives.

2

Adam and Eve

A Christian does not have to believe that Adam and Eve were historically the first two humans and that creation occurred in six days or even 6,000 years.

But Christians can believe that Adam and Even are symbolic figures, representing every man and woman, and that the creation story affirms that behind creation is design and plan.

3
God Speaking

A Christian does not have to believe that God at one time spoke audible words to Abraham, Moses, and the prophets.

But Christians can believe that biblical conversations with God represent that inner dialogue between the individuals and the divine will.

4
The Miracles of Moses

A Christian does not have to believe that at Moses' decree the Nile turned to blood and various plagues afflicted Egypt, contravening the laws of nature.

But Christians can believe that the Moses stories point to a remarkable figure in history and assert his powerful influence.

5
Angels

A Christian does not have to believe that angels were visible spiritual creatures, who spoke audible words to Mary and Joseph.

But Christians can believe that angels are the messengers in life whose presence and supportive help radically change life situations.

6
Virgin Birth

A Christian does not have to believe that Jesus was conceived as a biological miracle without a human father.

But Christians can believe that Jesus was unique and special, a one-of-a-kind representative of a higher dimension of life.

7
The Miracles

A Christian does not have to believe that the miracles told about Jesus' life and death were historical happenings.

But Christians can believe that the followers of Jesus experienced transformation, empowerment, and new life and used bodily health symbols to express the radical changes experienced, and that they fervently believed that his death had cosmic significance.

8
The Blood of Jesus

A Christian does not have to believe that the shedding of Jesus' blood has some miraculous power in itself.

But Christians can believe that blood is a symbol of life and that Jesus' life has had a powerful influence upon the world.

9
Jesus' Descent into Hell

A Christian does not have to believe that after he died Jesus went to hell to preach to the lost of the past.

But Christians can believe that those in the past are included in God's seeking love, and God's Christ activity is the same yesterday, today, and forever.

10
The Resurrection and Ascension

A Christian does not have to believe that Jesus' physical body was resurrected from the dead and later levitated, moving from earth up to heaven.

But Christians can believe that physical bodies are important; humans do not become disembodied spirits; Jesus' physical body and ours have spiritual significance; and the life of Jesus has been raised up over all lives as the exemplar.

11
The Coming Again

A Christian does not have to believe that the physical, flesh-and-blood Jesus is coming back to earth again.

But Christians can believe that further "comings" are not unrelated to the first, and that whatever comes will be in harmony with that humanity represented in the fleshly life of Jesus.

12
Life after Death

A Christian does not have to believe that life after death means a continued existence with consciousness of self and others.

But Christians can believe that our state after death is in the hands of a loving God, that we have no need for fear or apprehension, that in the all-encompassing love of God we shall never not have been.

13
The Trinity

A Christian does not have to believe that the Trinity is an accurate portrayal of the nature of God.

But Christians can believe that the Trinity has to do with the nature of how God has been experienced, instead of an attempt to describe the essence of God.

14
Satan

A Christian does not have to believe that Satan (the Devil) is an actual personal being causing the evil in the world.

But Christians can believe that Satan is a symbol of the opposition to God's purposes for human life.

15
Essential Christian Convictions

God is the object of faith, a transcendent dimension of life not amenable to our physical senses; and Jesus (called Christ) is the lens through which I see God.

A source of love exists in this world that transcends all the changing circumstances of our lives.

Faith (trust) in this source of love is justified in human experience.

Creation is good; the physical is a channel of the spirit; human life has eternal meaning; and each individual has a role to play in the ongoing human enterprise.

In spite of fading human memories and the physical inconsequence of any life, in the all-encompassing love of God, everyone is kept throughout eternity.

Christianity is basically a social entity that unites individuals in a community of faith which has symbols and stories that define the course of life and illuminate the meanings in the capricious nature of human existence.

Notes

1. Robinson, J.A.T., *Honest to God* (Philadelphia: Westminster Press, 1963), pg. 20.

2. Niebuhr, H. Richard, *Radical Monotheism and Western Culture* (New York: Harper & Brothers, 1960), pg.126.

3. Campbell, Joseph, with Bill Moyers, *The Power of Myth*, ed. by Betty Sue Flowers (New York: Doubleday, 1988).

4. Green, Fred Pratt, "For the Fruits of This Creation," stanza 3 in most modern hymnals.

5. Buechner, Frederick, *Wishful Thinking* (New York: Harper & Row, 1973), pg. 94.

6. Ibid., pg. 95.

7. Outler, Albert, ed., *The Works of John Wesley* Vol. 2 (Nashville: Abingdon, 1985), pg. 384.

8. Spong, John Shelby, *Resurrection: Myth or Reality* (New York: HarperCollins, 1995), ch. 1.

9. Eiseley, Loren, *The Star Thrower* (New York: Times Books, 1978), pg. 300.

10. Campbell, Joseph, *The Hero with a Thousand Faces* (Princeton University Press, 1968), pp. 105-109, 213-216.

11. Some of the material in this chapter is taken from my previous book, *The Faith Once Given—The Apostles' Creed Interpreted for Today* (Philadelphia: Westminster, 1978), ch. 6.

12. Ibid.

13. Lindsey, Hal, *The Late Great Planet Earth* (Grand Rapids: Zondervan, 1972).

14. Outler, op. cit., pg. 156.

15. Jackson, Thomas, ed., *The Works of John Wesley* XI, "Advice to a Soldier" (London: Wesleyan Conference Office, 1872; reprint Grand Rapids: Zondervan, 1958-59), 199 ff.

16. Dyson, Freeman, *Infinite in All Directions* (New York: Harper & Row, 1988), pg. 294 ff.

17. Outler, op. cit., pg. 377 f.

18. As quoted in "Context," August 15, 1998, pg.6.

19. As quoted in "Values & Visions," Vol. 25, No. 5, 1994, pg.10.

20. Kung, Hans, *On Being a Christian* (New York: Doubleday, 1976), pg. 73 ff.

21. Ibid., pg. 76.

22. Jackson, op. cit., V, pg. 296.

23. Ibid., XIV, pg. 334.

Bibliography and Recommended Reading

Christ in a Pluralistic Age, John B. Cobb Jr., Westminster Press, 1975. (The U.S.' foremost process theologian on contemporary Christology.)

The Christian Agnostic, Leslie Weatherhead, Abingdon, 1967. (Quite easy to read and delightfully written by an English Methodist.)

Common Sense Christianity, C. Randolph Ross, Occam Publishers, 1989. (Common belief questions with answers that will satisfy some.)

The Faith Once Given, George M. Ricker, Westminster, 1978. (The Apostles' Creed interpreted for today.)

The God We Never Knew, Marcus J. Borg, HarperSanFrancisco, 1998. (A Jesus Seminar scholar giving his own spiritual journey.)

Grace and Responsibility, John B. Cobb Jr., Abingdon, 1995. (Summarizes and defines a Wesleyan way of doing theology.)

The History of God, Karen Armstrong, Knopf, 1993. (A thorough survey of the idea and experience of God among Jews, Christians, and Muslims.)

Honest to God, J. A. T. Robinson, Westminster, 1963. (A very controversial book of the 1960s and an eye-opener.)

Meeting Jesus Again for the First Time, Marcus J. Borg, HarperCollins, 1995. (A fresh approach to discerning the difference between the pre-Easter Jesus of history and the post-Easter Christ of faith.)

On Being a Christian, Hans Kung, Doubleday, 1976. (The classic book on Christianity of the past twenty-five years and used as a textbook in my university class on Christianity.)

Resurrection: Myth or Reality, John Shelby Spong, HarperCollins, 1995. (Presents a reasonable and non-literal Christian faith.)

Sense and Nonsense in Religion, Sten H. Stenson, Abingdon, 1969. (Tough theological issues considered in a clear and penetrating way, but a little "heavy" for the non-theologically trained.)

Why Christianity Must Change or Die, John Shelby Spong, HarperCollins, 1998. (A personal testimony of faith in a God the language about whom must not be buried in old thought-forms and symbols.)

Why Religion Matters, Huston Smith, HarperSan Francisco, 2001. (A respected authority on world religious offers his testimony to religion as the primary humanizing force.)

About the Author

GEORGE M. RICKER is the former pastor of University United Methodist Church in Austin, Texas, and has taught at Southwest Texas State University and Austin Presbyterian Theological Seminary. He presently serves as seminar director in the University of Texas SAGE (Seminars for Adult Growth and Enrichment) and QUEST continuing-education programs. He is the author of *The Faith Once Given* (Westminster Press, 1978). He is also a lecturer, seminar leader, and newspaper columnist. His one-minute spots *Something to Think About* have been featured on Austin radio.